Stepping Up to
Supervisor

Stepping Up to Supervisor

MARION E. HAYNES

Revised Edition

Menlo Park, California

© 1991 Crisp Publications, Inc.
© 1987 Marion E. Haynes
© 1985 PennWell Books

Printed in Canada by Webcom Limited

CrispLearning.com

05 06 07 08   10 9 8 7

Library of Congress Cataloging-in-Publication Data

Haynes, Marion E.
 Stepping up to supervisor / Marion E. Haynes. – Rev. ed.
  p.   cm.
 1. Supervision of employees.   I. Title.
HF5549.12.H39 1991   91-58108
658.3'02 – dc20   CIP
ISBN 1-56052-112-0

Contents

Part III Working with Individuals

Part IV Working With Groups

Appendix Planning for Growth and Development

Preface

It happens every day. The setting changes, but the event is the same. Someone is selected and promoted to the position of first-level supervisor. Typically, the one selected is expected to make the change in job duties with little help or guidance.

A common way new supervisors deal with this change is to consider how supervisors they have worked for in the past handled the job. Using this as a starting point, they decide not to do some things that they saw as ineffective or inappropriate. They also decide to add other things that they consider appropriate and necessary in order to be effective but which were left out by their prior supervisors. This turns out to be a rather haphazard way of defining the supervisory role. It is severely limited by the types of supervision experienced in the past and the insight of the newly promoted person.

Stepping Up to Supervisor was written to make the transition from worker to supervisor easier for you. The book looks at key issues in a brief, straightforward way. Read it; then keep it handy and reread specific chapters as you face the situations they address.

WHAT THIS BOOK COVERS

The knowledge and skills required to be a successful supervisor fall into four categories: personal, interpersonal, technical, and administrative. This book addresses only the personal and interpersonal categories. You must either rely on the knowledge and skills you already have or search out what you need from other sources in the other two categories.

Personal Skills. Successful supervisors have certain personal skills that make them stand out from the crowd. These skills, often referred to as style, lead to self-confidence, which in turn causes others to have confidence in you. This is a fairly universal category. It does not matter whether you work in a factory, laboratory, store, warehouse, hospital, or an office. You must handle yourself and your job in a way that makes others want to be a part of your group. Because of this broad-based relevancy, some of the elements making up this skills category will be covered in Part II.

vii

Interpersonal Skills. By its very nature, the job of supervisor requires you to work successfully with other people. Not only are there members of your own work group to consider, but also there are other groups on whom you depend for goods and services. You must learn to work effectively with these people in order to be successful. This skills category is also fairly universal. It will be examined from two points of view—one-to-one skills in Part III and group-centered skills in Part IV.

Technical Skills. Successful supervisors know how to do the work that members of their group perform. They frequently are called upon to help solve work-related problems, to train new employees, and to monitor work methods, safety practices, and quality of out-put. All of these require a substantial knowledge of the technology of the group. Ordinarily, this skills category does not represent a problem for new supervisors because often they are promoted from a position of doing the work to one of supervising it.

Administrative Skills. To a new supervisor, the list of administrative duties seems endless. Budgets must be prepared and expenses must be monitored. Forms for all kinds of things—absence reports, accident reports, time sheets, purchase orders, personnel records—must be filled in and routed to the appropriate people. In addition, procedures and policies must be learned and followed.

This category often presents the most challenge. Each organization has its own way of doing things, so the subject cannot be covered adequately in a book. To develop your skills in this category, rely on your boss or another more experienced supervisor you work with. Then ask questions and make notes. Above all, do not put off doing the paper work. It will bury you if you do.

Marion E. Haynes
Springdale, AR

Stepping Up to Supervisor

Part I
Introduction

- **What's Different Now That You're Boss?**
- **How to Be an Effective Supervisor**

1

What's Different Now That You're Boss?

CHAPTER HIGHLIGHTS
- Seven duties of first-line supervisors
- Three key areas of responsibility for first-line supervisors

---

"Congratulations! We're promoting you to supervisor the first of the month. Things are going to be different for you after this. Welcome to the ranks of management!"

As you walk away from your manager's office, you feel very proud but also a little concerned. The words, "Things are going to be different . . . after this," keep echoing through your mind. In what ways will they be different? A couple of ideas occur to you:

- The work itself will be different. There will be more administrative work, more supervising, and more managing with less involvement in the activities of the work group.
- The responsibilities will increase. As a supervisor, you will be responsible for the work of others rather than just your own output.

THE WORK OF SUPERVISION

The following list summarizes generally agreed-upon duties of a first-line supervisor. Compare your activities with this list. Are you overlooking something?

Assign and distribute work. There is much to be done and only so many people available. You must set priorities on what will get done, organize the work into reasonable assignments to make the best use of your people's talents, and assign the work so that some individuals are not overloaded while others have little to do.

Monitor and control performance. In order to ensure quality work being done through safe work practices, you must get

3

out and see what is going on. Do not wait until someone complains or gets hurt before checking into what your people are doing.

Review and evaluate performance. You must decide who will be recommended for promotion, who will be recommended for a pay increase, and who will have to be laid off or fired. In order to be fair to everyone, these decisions must be based in part on peformance evaluation. Additionally, most people like to hear how their work is evaluated. Take time to let them know how they are doing.

Train and develop employees. Your experience is a valuable resource to your work group. Use it when problems or unusual things happen. On the other hand, do not get hooked into doing someone else's work. Use problems and unusual situations as training and development opportunities. Also see that new members of your group are properly trained on the job. Do not assume they know how to do their job right just because they have done similar work elsewhere.

Lead your group. Leadership is getting everyone working together to achieve a common goal. Work with your group to coordinate individual effort and to build interest in doing a job well. Leadership is demonstrated in the decisions you make, the people you hire, the way you train them, the discipline you maintain, and the example you represent to them.

Communicate. A supervisor must communicate in order to get the job done. Let your people know what is to be done as well as policies and decisions that affect them. Notify your boss of any problems you expect as well as the general level of morale in your group. Advise other groups of your needs from them and things your group does that may affect them.

Handle administrative duties. Keep paperwork and records up-to-date. Your job will be much easier if the information you want is current and readily available. Time sheets, work reports, supplies inventories, accident reports, and invoices are just a few of the items making up a constant flow of paper.

THE RESPONSIBILITIES OF SUPERVISION

The job of supervisor carries with it a lot of responsibility. Some people are able to accept this and do well. Others have

4

difficulty with it, which leads to unnecessary stress and poor performance.

Responsibility to management. When you accept the job of supervisor, you accept the responsibility for getting the work done on time within existing rules and policies and within budget. You are a member of the management team. Therefore, you are expected to support management and do all you can to see that the goals of management are realized.

These responsibilities often result in severe stress. Sometimes it seems that you are caught in the middle of a problem. There is not enough time or other resources to get the job done; goals or deadlines appear unrealistic. Your authority may be unclear. You may feel you are not supported by your manager. When these or other issues start building stress, recognize it and try to eliminate the cause or find release away from the job.

Responsibility to your work group. When you accept the job of supervisor, you also accept the responsibility of looking out for your people. You represent management to them. Therefore, you are expected to see that they are treated fairly. This means that they receive all of the benefits to which they are entitled, that they are considered for advancement when opportunities develop, and that they receive the recognition they deserve.

Responsibility to yourself. Not everyone is cut out to be a supervisor. Some people simply cannot take the stress created by the demands of the job. You have a responsibility to yourself to recognize your own limitations. If you accept the job, accept the responsibilities and fulfill them to the best of your ability. If you are unsure, give it a try. Then if you find it is too much, ask for a reassignment. If you know the job is not for you, say so. Many people have found rewarding, satisfying careers that do not include the responsibilities of supervision.

CONCLUSION

Top-flight, first-line supervisors are critical to a company's success. They represent the company's interests in getting the work done. They are the link between management and other employees in carrying out policies, plans, and directives. In fulfilling this role, you must work through others and depend upon those supervised for your own success.

Many people find supervising an exciting, challenging role. They enjoy the involvement and marvel at the successes of their group and its individual members. Other people find the demands too great.

The key ingredient for a successful supervisor is honesty, both with self and others. Be honest with yourself; can you handle the job? Then be honest with your manager about what is going on in your group. Do not try to hide your shortcomings or those of others. Finally, be honest with your people. Do not string them along or lie to them. Face issues squarely, openly, and honestly.

SUGGESTIONS
- Clarify your own duties and responsibilities by negotiating an understanding with your boss.
- Clarify the duties and responsibilities of members of your group by negotiating an understanding with each of them.

2
How to Be an
Effective Supervisor

CHAPTER HIGHLIGHTS
- The two dimensions of supervisory style and the resulting four supervisory style options
- The two dimensions of work group member maturity
- Suggestions for matching supervisory style to member maturity for maximum effectiveness

---

Effective supervisors achieve results. That is your prime responsibility. Without the delivery of a product or service to your customers, there would be no reason for your group to exist. This delivery of a product or service provides focus, direction, and purpose to your group. You achieve results by managing the resources provided you—the people, materials, facilities, information, time, and money.

While generating a product or service, a second result is also being produced. That is the impact of the work experience on members of your group. This morale, or satisfaction, dimension is every bit as important as the product or service generated by your group in terms of long term effectiveness. In the short term, production can be increased at the expense of morale. But, in the long run, productivity will suffer if employee satisfaction is neglected.

SUPERVISORY STYLE

One of the most significant ingredients in work group effectiveness is the style used by the supervisor. It has a direct and major impact on the morale within the group and thereby affects productivity in both the short and long term.

7

Dimensions of Supervisory Style

Two areas of involvement have been identified which are central to the concept of supervisory style. One focuses on the tasks to be done; the other focuses on relationships within the group.

Task-Centered Involvement. This involves organizing and defining the roles of group members by explaining what tasks each is to do as well as when, where, and how they are to be done.

Relationship-Centered Involvement. This involves the development of personal relationships between group members, welding the group into a cohesive team, and providing support, recognition, and reinforcement to the group and its members.

Supervisory Style Options

When these two areas of involvement are used as axes of a two-dimensional model, four supervisory styles are identified. (See which description most closely matches your views.)

Relationship-Centered Involvement	Relationship-Centered	Integrated
	Separated	Task-Centered

Task-Centered Involvement

A Two-Dimensional Model of Supervisory Style

Task-Centered. Task-centered supervisors tend to structure and direct the work of their group. They also tend to define and solve problems on their own. They usually operate from the position that they know best how to get things done. They tend to treat group members as individuals and make each one accountable for a specific set of responsibilities. Supervisors using this style often influence others through dedication to hard work. Through competence, personal example, or careful use of power they can effectively maintain output.

Relationship-Centered. Relationship-centered supervisors identify with their work group and strive for a helpful and secure work atmosphere. They use relationships and recognition to influence others—preferring to not use authority. They look for good points in people. They prefer participative decision making. Since relationship-centered supervisors see their job as primarily supporting and encouraging others, they spend considerable time talking and usually are good sympathetic listeners. They present a trusting and positive attitude. They favor pleasant working conditions where personal freedom and self-expression are encouraged.

Integrated. Supervisors with an integrated style try to structure work and involve others in the cooperative achievement of goals. They tend to involve others in decision making and influence performance by stressing accountability, performance, and discussion then providing feedback on results. They usually set high standards for performance and production and explain to the group what they are doing. These supervisors believe conflict can be resolved through open discussion. Supervisors using this style are seen by their work group as being personally interested in its members and their development.

Separated. Supervisors with a separated style frequently delegate and usually in broad, general terms. They are often seen as being fair and objective about people and events; they rarely become emotionally involved. They enjoy monitoring goals, output, or activities of others. They tend to spend little time developing people or pushing for output. They spend most of their time keeping informed and analyzing data.

SUPERVISORY EFFECTIVENESS

When appropriately used, each style can be effective. The challenge is to match the right style to the circumstances you face. The best way to do this is to consider the maturity level of each of your group members along two dimensions.

Job Maturity. Job maturity is the ability to do the job according to acceptable standards. In assessing this quality consider experience and training. Does the person know the job? Has he

9

or she been trained in how to perform at an acceptable level? Has the individual done the job at an acceptable level in the past?

Personal Maturity. Personal maturity considers the willingness to do the job at an acceptable performance level. In assessing personal maturity consider interest and motivation, willingness to take responsibility, and self-confidence. Does the person stay with a job until it is finished? Is he or she a self-starter? Can the individual properly prioritize work? Are necessary steps taken early enough to assure work being completed on schedule?

Group members low in both maturity dimensions will respond best to task-centered supervision while those high in both maturity dimensions will respond best to a separated style. Group members high in personal maturity but low-to-moderate in job maturity respond well to an integrated style. Those high in job maturity but low-to-moderate in personal maturity do well under relationship-centered supervision.

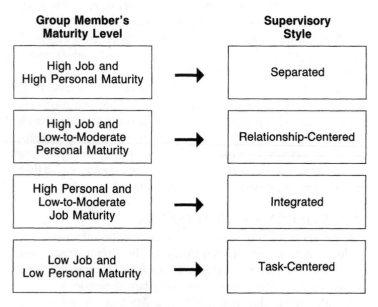

Group Member's Maturity Level		Supervisory Style
High Job and High Personal Maturity	→	Separated
High Job and Low-to-Moderate Personal Maturity	→	Relationship-Centered
High Personal and Low-to-Moderate Job Maturity	→	Integrated
Low Job and Low Personal Maturity	→	Task-Centered

**Matching Supervisory Style
to Group Member Maturity**

A natural application of this concept suggests a supervisor should start with a high degree of both task and relationship centeredness with a new group member. Taper-off on the task centeredness first, as the job is learned, and then taper-off on relationship centeredness to the point the new member is giving complete responsibility for a portion of the group's responsibility.

CONCLUSION

Clearly, you are responsible for producing results. But don't overlook the impact on morale you are having as you produce results. Because, in the long run, production will suffer if morale is low.

The most significant ingredient in the effectiveness of your work group is your supervisory style. No one style is effective in all situations. A task-centered style works best with group members low in both maturity dimensions. A separated style works best with group members high in both dimensions. The appropriate use of the other two styles is based on the group member's level of job maturity.

SUGGESTIONS
- Make a general assessment of morale in your work group.
- Evaluate the maturity level of each member of your group.
- Develop a plan to move each group member to the point where a separate style is appropriate.
- Don't neglect your responsibility to provide support, recognition, and reinforcement to your group.

11

Part II
Being Personally
Effective

- **Establishing Your Authority**
- **Communicating for Understanding**
- **Asserting Yourself**
- **Dealing with Conflict**
- **Dealing with Stress**
- **Planning Projects and Activities**
- **Managing Your Time**
- **Observing the Rules**

3

Establishing Your Authority

CHAPTER HIGHLIGHTS
- Six suggestions on how to get started as a new supervisor
- Recommendations for working with higher management
- Five ideas for working with a new group

The authority to supervise your group effectively does not come automatically with your promotion to supervisor; you must earn it. Three things will help you earn respect and authority from your group: ability to do your job, willingness to take necessary action, and equitable dealings with group members. With these three qualities as a foundation, you can build to establish your position as supervisor.

GETTING OFF TO A GOOD START

Your first few days as supervisor are critical to establishing your authority in the group. This period is marked by getting acquainted with the people and operations and letting the work group get acquainted with you. Do not attempt any major changes during this period. Your authority probably has not been sufficiently established to carry it out successfully.

Your boss can help you get started by personally introducing you to your work group and endorsing you as the supervisor. During this early period all of your boss's requests or directives should be channelled through you. This practice clearly marks you as the supervisor. Later on when you are established in the job, an occasional request directly to a member of your group from higher management will be okay.

Get Acquainted

Because you are the new supervisor, everyone is anxious to know who you are and what changes to expect. And, you need to know your people to work effectively with them.

Meet Everyone in the Group. Make a point during the first two or three days to meet everyone. This could be started as a group session but should include private discussions with each member of the group. During these discussions find out about each person's background and interests and determine individual views of the present way the group is operating. Also, share your background, your philosophy on supervision, and your expectations of the group.

Identify Informal Leaders. In strange situations you need a source of information to learn the rules of the game. This is necessary so you do not violate expectations of the group or trample on its traditions. Teaming up with the informal group leaders can accomplish this for you when they are willing to cooperate. Check out ideas you are considering to see how they might be best presented to the group. Ask questions about how things have been done in the past so you do not go contrary to established practices. By enhancing informal leadership, you win its support. In turn, your endorsement by informal leaders wins work-group support for you.

Circulate Among Group Members. You must get out of your work area and circulate among your group. This lets you see what is going on and helps you learn about the operation and any problems that exist. It also allows you to get better acquainted with group members. Frequent contact with the people and operations provides you with opportunities to answer questions and offer suggestions based on your knowledge of the work process. Members of your group will receive a sense of personal satisfaction just from the opportunity to talk to you and be acknowledged by you.

Getting Under Way

As you begin to assume control and direction of the work group, proceed with deliberate caution. You want to begin building a winning team.

Minimize Status Differences. Supervisors are respected when they do not insist on being different from the group. This is accomplished by having group members call you by your first name (this may be undesirable in the presence of clients or customers), by being readily accessible to group members without appointment, and by being willing to help when some crisis arises.

Set a Positive Tone. Express confidence in the group either to maintain a high level of contribution, if this has been the case, or to develop into a high contributing group. Openly express your willingness and intent to get involved and do whatever is necessary for the group to succeed. Clearly establish that you and the group succeed together; you are not there to succeed at the group's expense.

Start Small. You gain status and establish your authority by getting members of your group accustomed to following your directions. Do this by building an experience base. Move from the most easily accepted areas around work quality and quantity to the more potentially controversial areas such as working hours or work-group size. This approach minimizes the chances of confrontation by someone refusing your directions or challenging your authority before it is firmly established.

CONTINUING THE PROCESS

As you continue the process of establishing your authority, you must address relationships within your work group and demands from outside your group. This may be a fairly hectic period for you. You are new in your job, challenges may be made to your authority, and everyone seems to be making demands. Things should settle down as you gain confidence and are able to allow more autonomy and self-direction to group members.

Working with Outsiders

Nothing does more to establish your authority than your ability to handle outsiders—upper management, service departments, suppliers, and customers. You earn the respect of your group when you consistently prevent the outside world from making high-stress demands, pushing people around, and interfering with predictable, comfortable routines.

Supervisors frequently are caught between the demands of higher management and the expectations of work-group members.

17

Reconciling these conflicts is not a passive process. You may have to confront your management to get demands modified, or you may have to take the chance of reinterpreting the demands. Occasionally, you will have to defend members of your group—perhaps even cover up at times.

Most organizations have competition between departments or other subgroups for budgets and opportunities. The more powerful or forceful supervisors and managers typically come away with a larger share of the benefits. Your ability to deliver to your group earns respect and support. To do this means you must develop your skills in both formal presentation and informal manipulation of the system. Look to successful peer-level supervisors to learn how things really get done in your organization. Then do not hesitate to confront the system in pursuit of legitimate demands for your group.

Working with Group Members

Establishing authority with individual members of your group will require a combination of direct communication and certain pesonal qualities. The following ideas will prove helpful.

Communicate Clearly and Directly. When giving orders or making requests, use a direct, positive style of communicating. Avoid apologetic, accusatory, or half-hearted approaches. A whiny or exasperated tone of voice and excessive rationalization minimize your authority. On the other hand, tact is necessary and appropriate.

Be Persuasive. To be persuasive, you must understand the other person's interests, concerns, and desires. When you have done this, a relationship can be formed between what you want done and what the other person's interests, concerns, or desires are. This requires a two-phase discussion. During the first phase find out as much as you can about the other person's point of view. In the second phase establish a mutuality of interests. Point out how doing what you want done helps the other person achieve his or her goals.

Demonstrate Confidence. To establish and maintain authority, you need to have confidence in your own ability to be successful.

18

You must be able to see yourself carrying out the duties of the job successfully. Coupled with self-confidence is courage. Successful supervisors must have the courage to confront problems and work them through to a conclusion. Self-confidence and courage must not be carried to an extreme. Wisdom and discretion often dictate a moderated or selective approach to problems, while humility—under proper conditions—bolsters respect.

Take Action. Most work groups favor a supervisor who takes action. Establish your authority by doing things: making decisions, solving problems, pursuing opportunities. Do not be categorized as passive, indifferent, or lazy.

Be Persistent. Establish and maintain your authority by hanging in, not giving up, and insisting that your reasonable demands be met. Being persistent means clarity of command and simple repetition. Keep asking, talking, and explaining.

CONCLUSION

Most people recognize and accept the fact that someone is boss. So you have a base already present from which to establish your authority within the group. From there, authority is established by your actions. Get to know your employees. Offer your information and knowledge in solving work-group problems. Do not be afraid to call the shots when you understand the situation. On the other hand, if you do not understand the situation, admit it and seek out guidance from your boss, other peer-level supervisors, or experienced work group members.

Identify with your group and become a part of it. You have an important function in the group just as other group members do. Nothing is more frustrating to employees than a supervisor who acts as an outsider, seems more concerned with acceptance by higher management than by the work group, or is seen as passive, indifferent, or lazy.

Self-confidence, initiative, and persistence are necessary to make it happen. People like to be a part of a winning team.

SUGGESTIONS

- Gradually build your authority.
- Become acquainted with both the people and operations.
- Identify with your group and protect it from outsiders.
- Communicate clearly, directly, and confidently.
- Be persistent; insist upon compliance with your directives and requests.

Communicating for Understanding

CHAPTER HIGHLIGHTS
- A model of two-way communication
- Four suggestions for improving communications
- Three sources of distractions that interfere with listening
- How to go beyond words in search of full understanding

Supervisors spend more time communicating than any other single activity. Most of this time is spent in face-to-face discussions: talking, listening, and observing. Depending on who is involved, you may be relaying information, gathering information, pursuading, evaluating, counseling, and building, or maintaining morale. Unfortunately, these goals are not always achieved.

IT TAKES TWO TO COMMUNICATE

Effective communication depends upon two people working together. This point is often overlooked. Many people approach communication as though it were the simple process of one person telling something to another person. This theory fails to consider whether the other person is paying attention and is able to gain meaning from the words used.

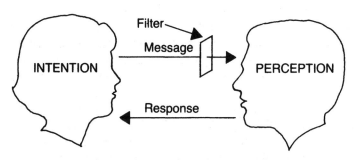

Two-way Communication Model

21

Moving to a more effective process requires getting the other person actively involved. The speaker can verify the listener's understanding by asking questions such as, "What is your understanding of what we've been talking about?" This process also makes it easy for the listener to get involved and clarify what the speaker is trying to communicate. Such questions as these would be appropriate: "Could you give an example of that?" or "Is this what you mean?"

When you develop the skill of active, two-way conversation, you will have taken a big step toward achieving understanding. However, three additional areas also need attention: removing filters, learning to listen, and learning to observe.

Remove Some of the Filters

Filters to understanding take many forms. The following suggestions should help you overcome some of the more common ones.

Do Not Assume Anything. How often have you said, "But I assumed that was what you wanted," when in fact something quite different was intended. Assumptions limit conversation and therefore limit understanding. Because something is assumed, it is never discussed. Check out your assumptions. They may be right, or they may be wrong. If they are right, move ahead with confidence. If they are wrong, correct them.

Watch Your Words. Words get their meaning from individual experience with them. Understanding requires that both speaker and listener have common experiences with the words being used. For this to happen, the speaker must think about the background and ability of the other person. A few things to keep in mind are education, age, work experience, and the area of the country the person grew up in. Use words the listener is familiar with. Keep it simple and don't use slang that will not be understood.

Build a Positive Climate. The climate or feeling two people share when talking determines how much communication takes place. The most important part of a positive climate is the amount of trust between the two. Employees will talk more with you when they feel they can trust you—that you will not embarrass them for what they say, use what they tell you against them, or pass on the information to others who should not know about it.

Pick the Right Place. All conversations should be held where those involved can be heard easily. Many conversations should not be overheard by other employees or customers. If the subject is personal, find a private place.

Learn to Listen

Listening is an active, engaging process of working with the speaker to develop ideas and achieve understanding. It requires concentration and a focus of attention and energy. Distractions from three sources often interfere.

Distractions in the Environment. These include noise and activity that make it hard to concentrate. Temperature and ventilation may cause drowsiness. Watch for these problems and eliminate them whenever possible.

Distractions Within You. Sometimes when you should be listening, you find your mind wandering. Other worries or concerns compete for your attention. The speaker may say something you do not agree with, and you start thinking about arguments against what was said. Concentrating on listening is the only way to overcome these distractions.

Distractions from the Speaker. Speakers frequently say or do things that are distracting. Some use too many words; others say "Uh" or "Okay" too often. Concentration and active involvement in the conversation will help avoid these distractions. Remember, valuable information can be stuttered, lisped, twanged, or delivered with beautiful clarity.

GO BEYOND THE WORDS

Much of a message's meaning is carried by the speaker's tone of voice and actions. An effective communicator observes these signs and gains understanding from them.

Tone of Voice

The voice represents the easiest clue to a speaker's feelings. Excitement, anger, joy, and frustration are just a few emotions that can be readily observed. Four qualities are significant:

emphasis, speed, pitch, and volume. When tuning in to voice tone, listen for two special cases. One is when the feelings being expressed are more important than the content. For example, an employee says, "I'll never be able to get it right!" Respond to the feeling of frustration rather than to the conclusion of failure. The other is when there seems to be a marked inconsistency between words and tone. For example, an employee speaking very slowly while agreeing with you is probably reflecting lack of agreement.

Nonverbal Communication

As you talk, observe what people do with their eyes, hands, arms, legs, and face. Direct eye contact typically communicates sincerity, confidence, and interest. Open, smooth gestures usually reflect an open attitude. Jingling or thumping something indicates nervousness or boredom. Is posture tense or relaxed? This is usually a clue to the amount of stress a person feels. Sitting relaxed but erect reflects confidence, while slouching indicates defensiveness. Folded arms may reflect suspicion or closed-mindedness. As with tone of voice, look for inconsistency between the words spoken and other behavior. If inconsistency is observed, check it out. Ask questions; seek out the true message.

CONCLUSION

Understanding can be achieved. However, to achieve understanding most people need to work on improving their communications. Supervisors in particular should recognize the importance of good communication skills and should work to develop them.

Face-to-face communications involve three channels operating at the same time: one carries words, another carries tone of voice, and the third carries body movements. To understand a message fully, all three channels must be received, blended, and interpreted. This requires careful attention and concentration. Two people must work together actively in pursuit of understanding, each checking along the way to make sure they are together.

SUGGESTIONS

- Use a two-way communication process to achieve understanding.
- Be thoughtful of the other person in the words you use, the setting, and your reaction to information received.
- Pay attention to what is said as well as how it is said and all nonverbal behavior.

5
Asserting Yourself

CHAPTER HIGHLIGHTS
- Three response alternatives available to everyone
- Four considerations in choosing a response
- Suggestions on how to handle five problem situations
- Four suggestions for controlling aggression

Effectiveness is the ability to get things done. Many people have talent. Good ideas are everywhere. But only those who can take ideas and turn them into results are considered effective. To do this requires assertiveness.

You assert yourself in three different arenas. First is the personal arena as you address your job duties, particularly the ones you consider tough to handle. The second arena is one-to-one interaction as you confront and work through problems you may have with others. The final arena is group interaction as you speak up in meetings to influence an outcome, either by supporting the current direction of the meeting or by introducing a new direction.

To be effective in both the one-to-one and group arenas requires that you be able to deal with others in a way that wins their support and cooperation.

RESPONSE CHOICES

When dealing with others, either individually or in groups, you have three choices for responding to situations.

Assertive. The assertive response lets you stand up for your rights without violating the rights of others. These rights include the right to refuse a request without feeling guilty or selfish, the right to make reasonable requests of others, the right to express yourself, the right to a fair deal, and the right to make mistakes.

To demonstrate your assertiveness, accept responsibility for your feelings, ideas, and actions; then speak up. State your needs and express your ideas and opinions. In the process, be sensitive and open to the needs, ideas, feelings, and opinions of others. The assertive response is honest, direct, expressive, and self-enhancing. When you are assertive, you make your own choices and feel good about yourself. Being assertive usually leads to achieving your goals. It also improves self-confidence and leads to freer, more honest relationships.

Passive. The passive response restricts your rights. You demonstrate passivity either by not speaking up or by giving in without developing an acceptable alternative.

The passive response usually is chosen to avoid unpleasant or risky situations—to steer clear of confrontation and conflict. Unfortunately, it has negative side effects. You do not get what you want. You are usually disappointed with yourself at the time and possibly angry and resentful later. This response is emotionally dishonest, inhibiting, and self-denying.

Aggressive. The aggressive response violates the rights of others. You demonstrate aggression either by ignoring others' needs, ideas, and opinions or by dominating others by making their decisions—telling them what to do and how to do it.

You choose the aggressive response to get your own way or to vent anger. In the short run it frequently leads to achieving your goals. However, it too has negative side effects. People on the receiving end of aggressive behavior often feel dominated, manipulated, intimidated, or humiliated. These feelings lead either to a desire to get even or to avoid future contact with the aggressor. Thus, you end up distancing yourself and developing enemies.

USING ASSERTIVE RESPONSES

The assertive response range demands active involvement with others. To be assertive, you must be willing to initiate contact and then initiate action. This requires at least a modest amount

27

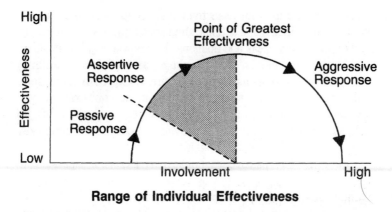

Range of Individual Effectiveness

of self-confidence. You must also be open in expressing yourself and open to the ideas of others.

Considerations

Not every situation calls for an assertive response. When deciding upon a response, there are four considerations:

- How is the course of events going? When things are going your way, support the proposed decision; when they are not, get actively involved in seeking an acceptable alternative.
- How important is the issue? Important issues call for more assertiveness. Issues may be important to you because of your values, what you stand to win or lose, or feelings of equity and fair play.
- How much do you know about the situation? When you are confident of your knowledge, you can be more assertive. When you feel others know more about the situation than you, be willing to accept their ideas.
- What is the power differential between you and the other person? When the other person is more powerful and might use that power to get even, know when to back off. For example, occasionally you might be less assertive with your boss than with a member of your group.

Problem Situations

Many situations can be handled in an effective way without creating undue concern. However, several general areas represent common problems: making and responding to requests, giving and receiving feedback, and handling aggressive behavior from others.

Making Requests. You have the right to make legitimate requests. You also have the right to express your own needs and expect a fair deal. The key to handling these situations effectively is being open to alternative ways of accomplishing your objective. For example, you have work that must be done on short notice, so you ask a member of your group to work overtime tonight. The individual responds that personal plans make it impossible to work overtime. What are the alternatives? Can another group member do it? Can this person come in early? Can someone from a temporary agency be brought in?

Responding to Requests. When others make requests of you, you have the right to express your needs and expect a fair deal. Again, the key is being open, exploring alternatives, and making a decision. Then say "yes" or "no" with conviction.

Giving Feedback. Many supervisors avoid giving feedback. To be effective in handling feedback, the approach is similar whether the feedback is positive or negative. Talk about the action or results, not the person. Then describe what happened and how you see it affecting your area of responsibility. During the discussion be specific; exactly how does something not measure up or where is it particularly good? When feedback is negative, encourage the employee to explore ways to do the work better; what needs to be done differently, and how should it be done?

Receiving Feedback. When receiving feedback, ask questions to clarify what you are being told. Remember, you want to be effective. If improvement is needed, be sure you understand what needs to be done differently and how it should be done. When receiving compliments, a simple "thank you" or expression of appreciation is all that is required. Do not play down your part in doing a good job.

Handling Aggressive Behavior. Handling aggressive behavior from others means you must maintain your self-control and consider the other person's feelings. If you are being ignored, as is the case when someone interrupts you, speak up and demand your rights. If someone's aggressiveness appears to be a venting of anger, express understanding for the feelings; then, when possible, move the person to a rational consideration of the problem. When someone seems unwilling to consider your needs or interests, attempt to delay the final decision. This gives both of you time to consider alternatives and potential areas for compromise. Be very careful about confronting aggressiveness in front of others. Demand a private setting and a cooling-off period if appropriate. Finally, consider what you stand to win or lose either by confronting or ignoring the aggressiveness. Select the approach that lets you come out best in the long run.

CONTROLLING AGGRESSIVE RESPONSES
When you move into the aggressive response range, individual effectiveness begins to decline. To operate at peak effectiveness, recognize what typically causes you to move into the range and develop an approach to prevent your becoming aggressive.

Causes of Aggressiveness
Generally speaking, aggressiveness is a response to conflict or stress. Therefore, it can be triggered by a variety of experiences. Conflict frequently results from opposition to what you want done or from someone encroaching on what you see as your area of responsibility. Stress results from such things as being caught in the middle of conflicting demands, having unclear responsibilities, being in a high-risk, unfamiliar situation, and having unrealistic goals or deadlines. (Other stress problems are covered in Chapter 7.)

Methods of Control
You can control aggressive responses by considering the situations that trigger them and deciding to respond assertively rather than aggressively. The following ideas will help increase your effectiveness.

Think Before Speaking. Frequently, a two- or three-second pause will give you enough time to consider the impact of what you are about to say to the other person. Especially in emotionally tense situations, it is important to choose words that do not increase the level of emotionality.

Change the Situation. If aggressiveness is a response to stress, work to change whatever is triggering it. For example, try to get your responsibilities clarified. Get goals and deadlines into realistic perspective. Improve the effective use of your time. Gain the knowledge and familiarity you need to do your job comfortably and well.

Try to Work Together. Do not be guilty of doing things that give others excuses for being uncooperative. Be flexible. Do not attempt to dominate others. And, within reason, be open to their ideas, suggestions, or requests.

Recognize Internal Signs. When experiencing stress, your body reacts. Some people perspire a lot; others get a knot in the pit of their stomachs or experience a tightening of the neck muscles. Pay attention to your body's signals and use them as a warning system. Then decide what to do to prevent a loss of effectiveness.

CONCLUSION

To be effective, you must be assertive. Assertiveness is the force that moves an idea from being a thought in your mind to becoming a product or experience. It is the key to getting results.

Assertiveness builds self-confidence and the admiration and respect of others. Passiveness results in a loss of respect from both self and others. The passive person tends to turn feelings inward and experiences anxiety, guilt, and depression. Aggressiveness builds enemies who are intent on getting even or aloneness as others avoid you.

Be flexible in your responses to situations. Every situation does not require an assertive response. Consider who is involved, the importance of the issue, and your knowledge of the situation. Then choose a response that lets you come out ahead. Remember, the goal is to achieve results, not to get your way or prove that you are boss.

SUGGESTIONS
- Express your ideas and opinions in a positive, straightforward way.
- Control aggression by working to minimize or eliminate its causes.

Dealing with Conflict

CHAPTER HIGHLIGHTS
- Suggestions for handling four common causes of conflict
- Five approaches to resolving conflict
- Two major concerns that influence approaches to resolving conflict

Conflict occurs when the desires of two people appear to be incompatible. How you handle these situations will have a dramatic impact on your ability to work successfully with that person in the future. Thus, two areas of concern always exist: your concern for winning your point and your concern for maintaining the relationship.

HANDLING COMMON CAUSES OF CONFLICT

Conflict is caused by: ineffective communications, and different perceptions, values, attitudes, and preferences. Each of these conflicts calls for a different approach to resolve it.

Miscommunications

Much conflict is experienced because people do not listen and understand each other. Someone says something that the other person interprets differently than was intended. Basically, there is no real conflict, but on the surface the misinterpretation can cause considerable distress.

This type of conflict can be avoided or at least minimized by better, more complete communication. Make sure you understand each other fully and accurately. Do not assume anything. Use enough context to assure understanding.

Different Perceptions

A very frustrating form of conflict develops when two people view the same situation and come away with different perceptions of the "facts." When you experience this form of conflict, be tentative in your position. Relationships can be damaged if you take too strong a stand, whether or not you are right.

Resolving this form of conflict can be handled in four different ways, depending upon the actual situation:

- Gather and present more information to support your position.
- Review the facts together to see where you begin to differ and try to clear up this difference.
- Agree on a third party, usually an expert, to go over the positions and decide which is correct.
- If the issue is a matter of record, look it up and see who is right.

Different Values

These differences grow out of individual value systems and people's attitudes based on those values. For example, an engineer or accountant might refuse to do certain things because of professional ethics.

This form of conflict can be addressed in two different ways. One is agree to disagree. This approach acknowledges that two people need not think the same in order to work together success-fully. Of course, this approach can only apply to those areas that are not part of the job. The other approach is to identify a higher value held by both people that will justify compromising the lower value difference. For example, respect for the law could be adequate justification though his value system tells him, "That's not proper work for a woman."

Different Preferred Outcomes

The basis for this conflict is that two people want different solu-tions to the same problem. It usually is a problem in which they share an interest. The problem may involve allocating a limited resource or it may simply be a situation where both have decided what they want to do.

With open communications, this form of conflict usually can be resolved by a joint problem-solving discussion. (See Chapter 22 on decision making.) To be effective, both parties must be willing to state their needs and concerns clearly then work together to find an alternative solution that meets these needs and concerns.

APPROACHES TO RESOLVING CONFLICT

The approach taken to handle a conflict situation can be examined from the two points of view mentioned earlier: concern for winning and concern for the relationship. The way these two concerns work together results in five different approaches to conflict, four of which are shown in the illustration.

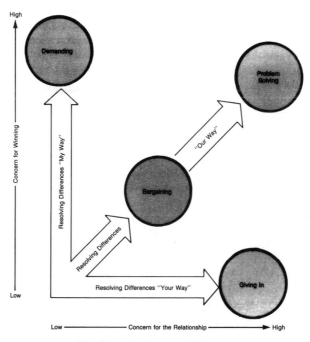

Conflict Resolution Model

Demanding

This approach to resolving differences suggests that winning your point is very important to you and that the relationship between you and the other person is unimportant. The objective

35

in demanding is to maximize one's own outcome. However, this usually is at the expense of the relationship because in demanding there is always a winner and a loser. Most people do not like to lose. When they do, they are often motivated to get even.

Demanding can be used appropriately to resolve differences where there is no need to work together in the future or where you need to protect yourself against those who might take advantage of you. It is also appropriate when the rules of the game dictate, such as in allocating limited resources or competing in the marketplace for a share of the business.

Problem Solving

Problem solving is high in concern for winning and concern for the relationship. It is characterized by both parties working together actively to find a mutually satisfactory solution. It requires joint problem solving, which in turn leads to creative solutions and commitment to carry them out.

Problem solving is appropriately used when there is a need to continue working together. It lets both parties leave the discussion feeling good about the outcome. It should be used to find solutions to joint problems, to merge insights of those with different perspectives on a problem, and to gain commitment by incorporating the concerns of others into the decision.

Bargaining

Bargaining is best described as a retreat or backup position when you are unable to reach a solution by demanding or problem solving. This position remains moderately high on each of the concerns. It is most effective when both parties are willing to give a little in order to achieve a resolution of their differences.

Bargaining is appropriately used when your goals are moderately important but are not worth further effort or when the relationship may be damaged from pushing your position further. It is often the only means of resolution when two equally powerful people are committed to mutually exclusive outcomes.

Giving In

In this response, maintaining the relationship is more important than winning the point. You simply agree to do what the other person wants. Giving in is appropriate when you realize you are wrong. If you are presented new information that invalidates your position, acknowledge it and support the solution suggested by the facts. Do not get caught defending a wrong position just to save face. Giving in is also appropriate when you realize the issue is more important to the other person than it is to you. This will help to build and maintain a cooperative future relationship.

Avoidance

Every conflict does not need to be resolved immediately. Avoiding confrontation can be appropriate when the issue is trivial or when you see no chance of satisfying your own concerns. It can also be used appropriately for a temporary delay so people can cool off and you can collect your facts. It is appropriate to avoid resolving side issues that would only take the discussion off the main topic. Finally, it is important for you to avoid getting involved in conflicts that do not concern you or conflicts that people can handle without your help.

CONCLUSION

Conflict is a part of life. When properly handled, it leads to better understanding and innovative solutions to problems. When it is not handled properly, it leads to hurt feelings and damaged relationships.

Conflict is caused by several different issues. Knowing the underlying cause helps suggest ways of clearing up the differences. Since miscommunication is a common cause of conflict, it is an appropriate starting place. Be sure you understand each other. If this does not clear up the differences, follow an approach to resolve the type of conflict that exists: different perceptions, different values, or different preferred outcomes.

37

The way people approach conflict can be analyzed from two perspectives: the degree of concern for winning a point and the degree of concern for maintaining the relationship. From this analysis, five different approaches emerge: demanding, problem solving, bargaining, giving in, and avoidance. Each is appropriate under the right circumstances. Frequently, however, people do not analyze conflict and choose an appropriate approach. The tendency is to use a comfortable strategy in all situations. This often leads to addressing concerns improperly and/or damaging important relationships.

SUGGESTIONS

- Openly address conflict between yourself and others with whom you must work.
- Be sensitive to potential damage to the relationship from pushing your point too strongly.
- Use a collaborative problem-solving approach to resolving differences between yourself and others you must work with.
- Be open in expressing your needs, concerns, ideas, and opinions.
- Listen to the other person's needs, concerns, ideas, and opinions.
- Be flexible in searching for a solution that meets the needs of both of you.

7

Dealing with Stress

CHAPTER HIGHLIGHTS
- A model of stress in perspective
- Four effective ways of dealing with stress
- Three ineffective ways of dealing with stress

Stress is a part of life today as it always has been. The causes of stress vary with changes in job assignments, such as promotion to supervisor, but the fact of stress itself does not.

Stress is the body's response to threat that in turn causes the individual to take action to reduce the threat. Under many circumstances this is a very positive experience. Creative and productive capabilities are energized to accomplish some worthwhile goal. Other times, stress leads to negative experiences. This occurs when it is not channeled toward a worthwhile goal or when there is too much of it.

STRESS IN PERSPECTIVE

Many day-to-day experiences of supervisors cause stress—deadlines, goals, interviews, conflict. For some, these experiences are well within the range of positive stress, while for others

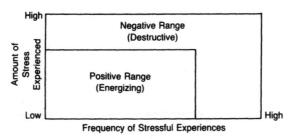

Individual Responses to Stress

they are in the negative range. Individual thresholds vary considerably; therefore, responding to stress must be approached on an individual basis.

When stress moves into the negative range, either because of a highly stressful experience or an accumulation of several less stressful events, a number of potentially harmful bodily reactions occur, including insomnia, loss of appetite, headache, ulcers, stroke, nervous tension, high blood pressure, and heart attack. In order to survive your job with some degree of satisfaction, you must learn to deal with the stress you experience. In dealing with stress, the goal is not to eliminate it completely. Rather, it is to control the amount of stress being experienced and develop proper channels for its release. In other words, learn to use the energizing force of stress without crossing the threshold into the destructive range.

DEALING WITH STRESS

People deal with stress in a variety of ways. Some ways are effective; others are ineffective. Avoid the ineffective ones and seek the most effective method for you to handle the stress you experience.

Ineffective Responses

An ineffective response does not solve anything and may in fact create problems greater than the stress being experienced.

Drug Abuse. Some people respond to stress by smoking too much, consuming alcohol, or using illicit drugs such as heroin, cocaine, marijuana, amphetamines, or barbiturates. This response option is ineffective because it leads to impaired judgment and risk of addiction as well as debilitating physical side effects.

Withdrawal. Some people respond to stress by withdrawing physically or psychologically from the situation. Physical withdrawal includes avoiding certain people, being absent from work, or, in extreme cases, quitting the job. Psychological withdrawal includes apathy, lack of interest and commitment, daydreaming, and lack of assertiveness. While these are very popular response techniques, generally they are ineffective because performance will suffer, resulting in greater stress.

Medication. Both prescription and nonprescription medications are used to alleviate the symptoms of stress. Aspirin, antacid tablets, sleeping pills, and tranquilizers enjoy a high degree of popularity. Treatment of stress symptoms with medication brings only temporary relief. It does not solve anything in the long run. Therefore, medication falls into the ineffective category.

Effective Responses

Effective responses to stress let you make changes that reduce the amount of stress being experienced or channel the relief of stress into positive areas.

Modify the Situation. This response is aimed at reducing the amount of stress being experienced. Start by identifying sources and situations that trigger stress for you. Then change the situation so the source of stress is eliminated or reduced. For example, if you experience stress caused by insufficient time or resources, try to get more resources committed to your area. If your responsibilities are unclear, try to get them clarified. If you are caught in the middle between conflicting expectations, try to work out a compromise between the two. Whatever causes you to move into the negative stress range, try to change it.

Maintain Your Health. You handle stress better when you are healthy. Sometimes when the pace of work is particularly hectic, personal health habits slip. Consider each of the three ingredients for good health—diet, sleep, and exercise. Do you eat a balanced diet without skipping meals or overeating? Do you limit your coffee consumption? Do you get sufficient sleep on a regular schedule? Do you get regular, vigorous exercise such as walking, jogging, tennis, handball, swimming, or cycling at least three times a week?

Accept Responsibility for Your Life. Some people experience stress and personal anguish because they feel locked into circumstances beyond their control. They do things that they believe are expected of them but which they do not enjoy. For example, they tolerate an unpleasant job because they need the money. Or they accept a promotion because it is the thing to do and they appreciate the recognition. They take on unnecessary responsibilities because they believe no one else will do them properly. It is important to be in control of your life rather than be a pawn to circumstances or the expectations of others. Decide what your goals are and what is best for you. Then accept responsibility for the decisions you make and the consequences of those decisions. Be your own person. Look out for your needs.

Learn to Relax. You cannot experience stress and relax at the same time. Therefore, if you learn to relax, you can reduce the amount of stress you experience. To relax, you need four ingredients: a quiet place, a passive attitude, something to occupy your mind and thereby divert it from focusing on problems, and a comfortable position. Many people find that a short nap during the day is a great way to relax. Consider your situation. Is it feasible to get away for 15–30 minutes of relaxation, perhaps at lunch?

Engage in Recreational Activities. Recreation literally is a rebuilding, rejuvenating, re-creating process. You need something in which you can become totally immersed, such as woodworking, painting, gardening, hiking, boating, fishing, or golfing. In selecting a recreational activity, three factors are important. First, it should be something you thoroughly enjoy—something where you lose touch with the passage of time. Second, it should represent a marked contrast to your job in terms of energy requirements. Someone with a very active job should select a less active hobby. People who are fairly inactive in their work should choose an active recreational endeavor. Third, the focus of attention range should also be in contrast to your job. For example, those persons who do close, detailed work should have a hobby that directs their attention into the distance, such as golfing, hiking, or sailing. Those whose attention is focused in the distance during the workday should consider wood carving, painting, or stamp collecting.

CONCLUSION

People vary considerably in their tolerance for stress. Yet everyone has a point where stress moves from a positive range to a negative one. High levels of stress lead to physical and mental illness. Therefore, dealing with stress in an effective way is aimed at keeping you from crossing the threshold into the negative or destructive range and suffering its potential ill effects.

Effective dealing means getting control of your life, making decisions, and pursuing courses of action to eliminate as many of the causes of stress as possible. Then, maintain your health and learn to relax. Finally, find appropriate activities for recreation.

Do not try to eliminate all stress. Some is necessary to energize creative and productive forces.

SUGGESTIONS
- Identify the sources and situations that produce stress.
- Change as many of them as possible to reduce the amount of stress you experience.
- Choose effective ways of dealing with the stress that remains.

Planning Projects and Activities

CHAPTER HIGHLIGHTS
- The six steps for getting something done
- Four steps in developing a plan
- A sample project planning guide
- Suggestions on how to use your calendar as a planning tool

To accomplish anything worthwhile you need a plan. Simple plans can be roughed out in your mind, but fairly elaborate plans require careful detailing on paper.

A plan serves several purposes. First, it outlines what is to be done and the order in which the steps must be taken. Therefore, it becomes a road map to follow to reach a goal. Second, it lets you know when something must be started in order to be completed on time. Therefore, it reduces much of the pressure often caused by deadlines. Finally, it is an energizing force. When you have a goal and a plan to achieve it, you are more likely to succeed.

HOW TO GET SOMETHING DONE

In completing anything, there are usually six major steps. Occasionally, the list can be shortened—for example, when you are the only one involved.

Study the Situation and Select a Method

The starting point for any plan is to study the situation and to select a general approach for completing the job. During this step the problem should be clearly defined and a goal set. The goal should be a clear statement of end results to be achieved. Then a general approach or method for achieving the goal is determined. This is the opportunity to introduce creativity into the process. Expand your range of vision to include a variety of possible alternatives; then select the most feasible course of action.

Gain Agreement and Support

With the problem identified, the goal set, and a general approach selected, it is time to get others involved. Whose agreement and support do you need—boss, subordinates, other departments, other peer-level supervisors? Select the appropriate people and review your plan with them. This will ensure their cooperation when you need it later on. (Essentially, this step says, "Don't waste time developing detailed plans unless you have the necessary agreements to move ahead.")

Develop Your Plan

With general agreement, you can now do the detailed planning necessary to accomplish your objective. Four steps are involved.

Divide Your Plan into Steps. What are the tasks and activities that must be fulfilled to achieve your objective? Judgment is required to recognize the appropriate degree of detail at this point. Do not be either too general or too specific.

Determine Resources Required. Limited resources must be allocated on the basis of priorities. The two limited resources for most people are time and money. Therefore, these become the focus of attention in the planning process. Look at each step in your plan. How much time will be required to complete it? Consider your time, the time of others, and machine time, as appropriate. Think about two viewpoints: actual time required to complete the step and scheduled time required to complete the step, taking other demands and commitments into account. Do the same for money. What will it cost to complete each step?

Identify Any Sequences. With a breakdown and budget completed, study relationships among the steps to see in what order things must be done. Also identify tasks or activities that can be underway at the same time.

Develop a Schedule. From the time allocations, develop a schedule for completing your total plan. Look at steps that can be done at the same time and take this into account in determining your overall schedule.

45

SAMPLE PROJECT PLANNING GUIDE

Project: Publish a revised edition of *Managing by Objectives Workbook* by March 31, 1992.

Step	Est. Time	Schedule	Responsible
1. write draft	30 hr	15 days	author
2. type draft	16 hr	10 days	secretary
3. proof draft	10 hr	5 days	author
4. make corrections	3 hr	1 day	secretary
5. revise cover	2 hr	5 days	artist
6. type manuscript	12 hr	10 days	secretary
7. proof manuscript	10 hr	3 days	author
8. make corrections	3 hr	3 days	secretary
9. draft figures	6 hr	5 days	artist
10. proof artwork	1 hr	–	author
11. print and bind	8 hr	15 days	printer

Overall schedule: January 4, 1992 to March 31, 1992

Test and Review Your Plan

Before moving ahead, review your plan with someone and, in the process, test it. You can find an appropriate person either within or outside of your group.

Within Your Group. Review your own plans. To be effective, let them sit for a few days; then go back over them. A peer-level supervisor could be a good reviewer, especially one who has knowledge and experience in the type of work covered by your plans. An experienced employee in your work group could likewise serve as a reviewer. Your boss probably has some good ideas on how your plan can be improved.

Outside Your Group. You can consider two general areas outside your group. If you are doing a project for someone, that person becomes an appropriate reviewer of your plans. If other persons have a hand in completing your project, they should review at least their portion of your plan.

Implement Your Plan

Now put your plan to work. As you progress toward your goal, it is unlikely that everything will go smoothly. Be open to events as they develop and revise your plans as required. When deadlines are not being met, several courses of action are available: try to save time in some downstream step, bring in more resources (people, equipment, overtime), find alternative sources, settle for less than you originally expected, or negotiate a new target completion date.

Follow Up with Those Involved

If you have assigned portions of your plan to others, follow up with them to see that they are doing their part. Use your experience with an individual to decide how much follow-up is required. If someone has always delivered as promised, you may not need to follow up. However, with those who habitually fail to deliver or with whom you have no prior experience, follow-up—considering both timeliness and costs—is necessary.

USE YOUR CALENDAR

To bring some degree of order to your day, use your calendar to record starting and ending dates for each of the steps in your work plans. Also record on your calendar due dates for additional tasks that arise along the way, such as budgets, performance appraisals, staff meetings, and special reports.

Most people find it helpful to identify two time horizons relative to their work—a longer time period wherein general plans are made, along with details requiring substantial advance planning, and a shorter time period wherein final details are handled. For example, a longer time horizon might be two or three months; a shorter horizon might be one week. Within these periods, note on your calendar the things that must be done so you can handle them in a timely manner.

CONCLUSION

Planning is needed to accomplish anything worthwhile. It is the means for translating goals into reality. Planning provides direction

47

and motivation. It also relieves the stress associated with limited resources, principally time and money. With proper planning you can start early enough on a project to be sure of having sufficient time and money to complete it. Finally, day-to-day planning, within the context of a dual time horizon, will make a substantial contribution in bringing order to your day.

> ### SUGGESTIONS
> - Identify your time horizons.
> - Develop detailed plans for each significant project or goal.
> - Use your calendar to alert you when action needs to be taken.

9

Managing Your Time

Have you ever wished for more time? Few people seem to have enough, yet everyone has all there is. The problem is not a shortage of time but how you choose to use what you have.

In managing the use of your time, begin by looking at how you currently use it. Then see which of the suggestions for better time management will help you.

You will notice several results of better time management. First, you will get more of the really important things done, probably in less time. Then you will be able to get to those things that you seem to put off constantly. Finally, you should be able to find the necessary time to relax, reflect, and think.

USING YOUR TIME EFFECTIVELY

Since everyone has the same amount of time, the key question is, "Are you using your time effectively?" You should spend your time on things that only you can do and that result in the greatest contribution to your area of responsibility.

Find Out How You Spend Your Time

Before you can successfully gain control of your use of time, you need to know where it goes.

Analyze What You Do. Examine the work you currently do. Are you doing some things that are unnecessary? Some people spend time maintaining records and files that are never used. Are you doing work that should be done by someone else? If so, turn

49

it over to the appropriate person. Again, some people duplicate the work of others because they do not trust the ones who are primarily responsible to do a good job.

Consider a Time Log. Another way to evaluate how you use your time is to keep a time log of a typical week. Using the accompanying example as a starting point, design a log sheet that fits your particular type of work. Then, before going to lunch and before going home, record your daily activities. After a week examine your time log and analyze it for repetitive interruptions and activities that could be delegated to group members.

TIME LOG		
Time	Activity	Comments
7:00		
8:00		
9:00		
10:00		
11:00		
12:00		
1:00		
2:00		
3:00		
4:00		
5:00		

Establish Priorities

When you are satisfied that you are doing necessary work that only you can do, the next step is to set priorities. By setting priorities, you make sure that the important things get done first.

Make a List of Things to Do. One fairly simple but straight-forward system for prioritizing the use of your time is to prepare a list of things to do today. Some people make their lists at the end of the day for things to do tomorrow. Others make their lists each morning. (If you are in a car pool or use public transportation, this is a good way to use commuting time.) Be sure the list is in priority order. Then start at the top and work as far down the list as you can during the day. Anything left at the end of the day is carried forward to tomorrow's list and is reprioritized along with any new items.

Do Not Delay Things. Sometimes you may put things off that you know should be done but that you cannot motivate yourself to start. When this happens, consider the following ideas:

- Set a deadline for yourself to complete the task and stick with it.
- Set up a reward system. For example, "When I finish that task, I'm going to buy myself a new _____." Or "I'm not going to lunch until I finish this task."
- Arrange with someone (an associate, secretary, etc.) to follow up with you on your progress.
- Do the undesirable task first in the morning and be done with it.

Learn to Say "No." In some cases, the demands on your time will exceed your ability to accommodate all of them. Here is where priorities and the ability to say "no" can come to your rescue. When you take on more than you can handle, quality usually begins to suffer. In the long term, you will be better off to take on only what you can handle well.

Saying "no" does not have to offend someone. (See Chapter 5 on assertiveness.) When you can offer an alternative, things can usually be worked out to everyone's satisfaction. On the other hand, when a new demand comes in that is higher in priority than some of your current commitments, renegotiate the due dates on your current projects or have them reassigned to someone else.

Get Organized

You can make the most effective use of your time by getting organized. This prevents time from being wasted on looking for things or starting for the second or third time.

Organize Your Work Area. Is your work area cluttered? Do you spend valuable time looking for things? Take a few minutes and consider how often you have referred to each item you have on your desk. Those things you have not used in some time should be filed and indexed in a convenient place. Your work area should be organized so it is easy for you to complete your normal tasks.

Organize the Use of Your Time. Avoid diversions and interruptions to the extent that you can. Many people do this by scheduling an hour of quiet time each day. Depending on the nature of your work and your preference, the quiet hour can be either in the morning or afternoon. (Some find it necessary to come to work an hour early or stay an hour later in the evening.) During your quiet hour avoid interruptions by closing your door, turning off the phone, etc. Then concentrate on whatever needs your attention.

Another contribution to organizing the use of your time is to practice task completion. When you have too many things in progress at the same time, you lose time moving back and forth among them. Set your priorities; then move through the work to be done in an orderly way.

LEARN TO HANDLE COMMON DISTRACTIONS

Even when you are well organized and try to use your time effectively, there will be interruptions and distractions to contend with. Here are some ideas for handling the three most common ones.

Drop-in Visitors

Controlling the time taken up by drop-in visitors requires both courtesy and good judgment. As a starting point, limit the number of people you invite to your work area. If you need to be with someone, go to his or her work place. This way, you can control your time commitment by simply excusing yourself and leaving when you have accomplished your purpose. It is much more difficult to get people to leave your work area than it is for you to leave their's.

You can head off many drop-in visitors by turning your desk so your back is to the door. When people walk by and see that you are busy, they tend not to interrupt you unless it is important to do so. Consider closing your door, if you have a private office, when you need to concentrate. Again, the casual drop-in will think twice before interrupting you.

Finally, when someone drops in, stand up to talk. Do not invite your visitor to be seated unless you have time to spend in conversation. Usually when you stand, your visitor will also remain standing. This will significantly limit the length of the conversation. If this does not work, just be tactful and honest with your visitor. Consider something like, "Thanks for dropping in. However, I really need to get this project finished."

Telephone Calls

For many people, telephones are a constant interruption that you probably cannot eliminate. The best you can hope for is to limit the amount of time they take. If you have someone to answer your phone, you can screen out a few calls that should be handled by someone else and have calls taken during periods when you should not be interrupted.

When talking on the phone, do not initiate social conversation unless both you and the other person have time for it. Do not go into unnecessary elaboration in response to questions. End the conversation when it has achieved its business purpose. Do this in a polite but firm way by saying, "Thanks for calling. I'm glad I could be of help." Or "Thanks for calling. I have something I must get back to."

Incoming Mail

A third way others enter your life and make demands on your time is through the mail. Unsolicited business mail, often called junk mail, arrives daily in an unending flood. If you have someone to sort your mail, give that person guidelines on what you want to see, what should be routed to others, and what should be

53

thrown out immediately. The mail you see could then be sorted into two categories: "information only" and "action required." Establish a practice of handling each piece of mail only once. As you read it, decide what action is required and then proceed. "Information only" mail can be accumulated and read at convenient times. These times might include when commuting, while waiting for appointments, while waiting for meetings to begin, over lunch, or in the evening.

You can save a lot of time responding to mail by telephoning with requested information, having someone else telephone and pass on the information, or by writing a brief response in longhand on the original letter and mailing it back. If a record copy is needed, have the letter with your reply on it photocopied before it is mailed.

CONCLUSION

Everyone can use their time better. Look at how your time is presently being used. Be sure you are doing necessary work that only you can do. Set priorities; then learn to say "no" to demands of low priority that overload you. Trade off low-priority commitments for high-priority ones that come up unexpectedly.

Provide time in your schedule for the unexpected. You cannot anticipate everything that will happen, so leave some time each day to handle crises. Use your own experience as a basis for estimating the number and types of crises to expect. Then develop some contingency plans for handling them. This is the first step in getting off the merry-go-round and changing from a reaction mode of operation to a planning mode.

SUGGESTIONS
- Eliminate all unnecessary work you are now doing.
- Delegate all that you can to other members of your group.
- Prepare a list of things to do each day.
- Learn to say "no" when you reach your capacity to maintain quality performance.
- Organize your work area for greatest efficiency.

10

Observing the Rules

CHAPTER HIGHLIGHTS
- Suggestions on administering company policy
- Suggestions on operating within a labor contract
- A summary of five federal laws
- General considerations under state and local laws

In most organizations, rules exist to ensure the well-being of the company and its employees and to provide fair and equal treatment for all. Additionally, federal, state, and local laws protect the rights and safety of employees. As a supervisor, you are expected to operate within these rules and the law. Yet it is not uncommon for a supervisor never to be told about them. Therefore, individual supervisors are responsible for checking the rules that affect their decisions and actions.

COMPANY POLICY

Company policies, rules, or practices normally exist to cover frequently encountered events. They typically are formulated to save time deciding common issues and to see that employees experience similar treatment in similar situations.

Typical Areas Covered

Policies often specify the details of benefit plans such as vacations, insurance, and pensions. There usually are policies detailing the procedures for handling employment, salary administration, promotions, and training and development. Finally, policies often cover hours of work, procedures for days off, and limitations on days off with pay, such as sick leave and personal leave.

Rules usually cover employee behavior. They typically specify what employees are expected to do and describe penalties for violating the rules. Areas covered include procedures for advising supervision of absences, restrictions on leaving the work site during working hours, penalties for gambling, drinking, or fighting on the job, and requirements on working overtime. Many rules are unwritten, such as rules against stealing or striking a supervisor. Unwritten rules have the same effect as written ones.

Responsibilities of Supervisors

Supervisors have responsibilities in three areas regarding company policies, rules, and practices: they should know what the policies are; they should administer rules fairly and equitably; and they should voice their ideas about changes in the policies or rules to keep them up-to-date.

In administering policy, three general categories of policies can be distinguished. One category includes benefit plans. Supervisors ordinarily are not expected to know the details of these. It is usually sufficient to know that a plan exists and to know the personnel officer or plan administrator to whom people can go for details. The second category includes policies on hours of work, absences, and pay practices. Supervisors should know the details of these. You are expected to administer these policies fairly and consistently. The third category includes policies that do not ordinarily affect supervisors directly, such as employment practices. Here, for example, the employment office is directly responsible for following these policies.

LABOR CONTRACTS

Frequently, employees join together and negotiate a contract with their employer. When a labor contract exists, it represents another set of rules affecting supervisory practices.

Typical Areas Covered

Labor contracts cover wages, hours, and conditions of employment. This typically means that wage rates are specified for job classifications covered by the contract, work days and work weeks are defined, and conditions requiring premium pay are specified, such as overtime, call-in, or holiday premiums. Under conditions of employment, the three most common provisions are promotions procedures, layoff procedures, and grievance procedures.

Responsibilities of Supervisors

If employees in your work group are covered by a labor contract, it is your responsibility to read it, understand it, and abide by its terms. The key to labor contract administration is the intent of the parties when the contract was negotiated. This occasionally means that a contract provision will not be applied literally. Past practices may become the most reliable basis for interpretation and administration. New supervisors in particular should spend some time making sure they understand the intent and application of the contract. If differences of opinion occur over contract interpretation, check with the labor relations officer or labor attorney to determine the company's position on the issue in dispute.

FEDERAL LAWS

Many federal laws exist to protect the rights of employees and provide for their health, safety, and welfare. Some apply to specific industries; others are more general. Summarized here are the five major laws with the broadest coverage. Do not assume, however, that these are the only laws that may apply to you and your organization.

Fair Labor Standards Act

Through amendments to the original law, this act's coverage has been extended to most American workers. It covers those persons engaged in interstate commerce, involved in the production of goods for interstate commerce, or employed by a firm engaged in any of these activities.

Provisions. This law has four major provisions. The first specifies minimum ages for employment. No one under 18 years of age may be employed in hazardous occupations; no one under 16 years of age may be employed in manufacturing and mining activities; and no one under 14 years of age may be employed under any conditions. The employment of 14 to 16 year olds must not interfere with their schooling, health, or well-being. The second major provision specifies minimum wages for doing work regardless of where or when it is performed. This includes

57

changing clothes and washing when required, and attending meetings directly related to the employee's work when attendance is required. The third provision requires overtime pay at the rate of 1½ times the base rate for all hours over 40 in a work week. (The law provides for exemptions based on the nature of work. Basically, professional, administrative, supervisory, and managerial employees are exempt.) The fourth major provision was added in 1963. It prohibits wage differentials based solely on sex.

Responsibilities of Supervisors. As a supervisor, your major responsibility under this law is to see that employees are paid properly for all hours worked. For example, if an employee puts in extra hours without being asked to do so, he or she is still entitled to wages for those hours. If you ask employees to take work home, they are entitled to pay for the hours worked unless exempted from the law. Your other area of responsibility is to see that men and women doing similar work are paid the same.

Civil Rights Act

Through executive orders and additional laws applying to specific groups such as veterans and handicapped people, the provisions of this law are extended to nearly all workers. It covers employers with 15 or more employees and contractors doing business with the federal government.

Provisions. These laws require that there be no discrimination in employment or the conditions of employment due to race, color, religion, sex, national origin, age, physical or mental handicap, or veteran status. There are also restrictions against sexual harassment by making it illegal to extend or deny privileges and opportunities in exchange for sexual favors. Finally, federal contractors must take positive steps to see that their work force reflects the ethnic and sexual mix of the available applicant population.

Responsibilities of Supervisors. Your role under these laws is to ensure that there is no discrimination, either favorably or unfavorably, in your work group. Occasionally, this may mean you will have to take a strong stand against the wishes of your group to ensure the fair treatment of one of its members. The law, on the other hand, does not require you to keep employees who are not doing their job. It only requires you to be fair and consistent with everyone.

Americans with Disabilities Act

Until July 26, 1992 this act applies to employers with 25 or more employees engaged in an industry affecting interstate commerce. After that, the number of employees drops to 15.

Provisions. As far as employers are concerned, this law has two major provisions. It prohibits discrimination against qualified individuals with physical or mental disability in employment and all the privileges of employment. It specifically prohibits pre-employment examination or inquiry about a disability or the severity of a disability except as it might relate to performing job-related functions. Within certain guidelines examinations may be required after an employment offer and prior to reporting to work.

Additionally, it requires employers to make reasonable accommodations in facilities, job content, work schedules, equipment, and training materials that do not constitute an undue hardship for the employer. It also requires that qualified readers and interpreters must be provided when required due to the nature of the disability.

Responsibilities of Supervisors. Basically, it is your responsibility to see that there is no discrimination based on disability in your work group. Specifically, you must not make any illegal inquiry of applicants and you must make all reasonable accommodations to work effectively with a disabled member of your group.

National Labor Relations Act

This law covers employers whose business affects interstate commerce. It gives employees the right to organize and bargain collectively concerning their wages and working conditions. Subsequent laws in this area cover the conduct and activities of unions and employers to protect the rights of employees.

Provisions. The law grants employees the right to unite and act collectively concerning wages and working conditions. (This right has been interpreted to extend to informal collective activity as well as activity involving unions.) It sets up procedures for determining union representation by secret ballot and states rules governing the procedure to ensure freedom of choice. It restricts certain behavior classified as unfair labor practices that interferes with employees' rights under the law and their freedom of choice. For example, an employer can express views and opinions on the value of a union but may not threaten, promise, or interrogate employees concerning membership. The law also establishes administrative procedures for determining violations of the law and for assessing remedies and penalties.

Responsibilities of Supervisors. Your responsibility under this law is to avoid committing an unfair labor practice. Basically, that means you are not to interfere with employees' rights to organize and engage in concerted activities for their mutual aid or protection. You are not to dominate or interfere with the formulation or administration of any labor organization. You are not to encourage or discourage membership in any labor organization or discriminate against employees for the legal exercise of their rights.

Occupational Safety and Health Act

This law affects virtually everyone. It covers any employer (one or more employees) engaged in a business affecting interstate commerce. The employer must provide a place of employment free from recognized hazards likely to cause serious injury or death and must comply with health and safety standards issued under the law.

Provisions. This law gives the Department of Labor the right to establish health and safety standards for various industries. It provides a means for obtaining variances from standards that do not present a hazard to employees. It allows the inspection of company facilities by compliance officers from the Department of Labor and provides for citations and penalties for violations of the law.

Responsibilities of Supervisors. Your responsibilities under this law include ensuring a safe work place by making periodic inspections and correcting potential hazards. You are responsible for seeing that members of your group follow safe work practices. You are also responsible for abiding by or obtaining variances from the safety and health standards established under the law. Finally, you are responsible for providing appropriate safety equipment and enforcing its use.

STATE AND LOCAL LAWS

State and local laws cover three general areas: they extend federal laws to employers not specifically covered by the federal law, they are usually more specific regarding the employment of children, and they provide for the welfare of workers through benefits such as workers' compensation for on-the-job injuries and unemployment benefits. Responsibilities include reporting all on-the-job injuries. If you supervise workers under 16 years of age, be particularly aware of your obligations under the laws of your state. Usually there are restrictions on the number of hours per day, when the hours occur, the nature of permissible work, and appropriate wage levels.

CONCLUSION

There are several rules to learn in order to carry out your supervisory responsibilities fairly and equitably. Know your rights and obligations under company policy, labor contracts, and federal, state, and local laws. Some general themes run through all of those: be fair, be consistent, do not interfere with employees' rights, do not coerce or intimidate employees, do not discriminate, provide a safe work place, and be particularly cautious if you employ workers under 16 years of age.

SUGGESTIONS
- Read and understand the policies and rules you are expected to administer.
- If your work group is covered by a labor contract, read and understand its application.
- Apply policies, rules, and labor contract provisions fairly and equitably.
- Operate within the law. When you are not sure, check with your boss or appropriate staff personnel.

Part III
Working with
Individuals

- Working Through Others
- Providing Feedback
- Training Your Staff
- Evaluating Performance
- Reviewing Performance
- Handling Performance
  Improvement
- Handling Discipline
- Handling Terminations

11

Working Through Others

CHAPTER HIGHLIGHTS
- A model for understanding influence
- Three bases of influence available to supervisors
- Seven things supervisors can do to encourage good performance

Most work gets done by interested people working together in a spirit of cooperation. Occasionally, this system breaks down. For some reason, the work group or one of its members seems to lose interest, cooperation disappears, and performance suffers. To many supervisors, this becomes one of their most difficult challenges.

There are no magic answers that assure success in getting others to do as you want. Some general principles have been successful when applied to large numbers of people. However, every person has the choice of either doing or not doing what you ask. You are only one voice. At any point in time, other voices guiding that person's decision may include family members, others in the work group, and inner voices, such as self-image, interests, values, and needs. (See figure.)

Internal Forces		External Forces
Self-Image		Supervisor
Needs, Wants, Desires		Peers
Abilities		Family
Values		Rules, Norms, Laws
Interests		Setting

Forces Influencing Behavior

BASES OF INFLUENCE

As supervisor, you have three important bases from which to operate in your efforts to gain cooperation. Consider the extent to which you use each of these. Effective supervisors develop and use all three.

Position. Because you are supervisor or boss, you can make requests and issue orders. Most of the time, those reporting to you will do what you ask or tell them to do. This is a fact of work life that most people accept—when you work for someone you do as they say. Also as boss, you have the ability to reward good performance and punish poor performance. Most work-group members will do what is expected in order to receive the rewards and avoid the punishments.

To maintain this source of influence as an effective force in your work-group, you need to know and operate within your limits and be fair and consistent in its use. Do not make inappropriate or unreasonable demands. Do not promise rewards or threaten punishments you cannot or do not intend to deliver.

Knowledge. Because of what you know, you can influence how others do their work. From your experience, you may have a special skill or you may be the only one who knows how to do certain tasks. When this fact is generally known, others will come to you for advice or guidance. Through the use of your knowledge, you can then influence them to do their work better, easier, or safer.

To maintain this source of influence, you need to keep up-to-date in a knowledge area that is important to the group. You also need to maintain a good track record by being available when needed, communicating your knowledge and providing advice and guidance that get good results.

Relationships. Because of your relationship with members of your group, you can ask and receive certain performance. Most people are willing to do what a friend asks. This is usually based on a sense of mutual cooperation. This spirit of working together is fostered by acknowledging people, doing favors for them, and helping them.

To maintain this source of influence, build a relationship with each group member. Get acquainted. Show an interest in them. Help when you are needed. On the other hand, do not take advantage of anyone. Do not ask for anything that is beyond the limits of a proper relationship, for example, something illegal, unethical, or in violation of personal values.

WAYS OF WORKING THROUGH OTHERS

Using these three bases of influence, you can develop several ways of working with the members of your group to get them to carry out willingly the responsibilities of their jobs.

Clarify Expectations. The starting point for building an effective work group is to be sure everyone understands what you expect. Do not assume they know. Discuss it. When clarifying job expectations, be open to ideas the other person has about what is to be done or how it should be done.

Provide Feedback. Let people know how they are doing. Tell them when they do something well and also tell them when they do something poorly. Think of feedback as building a road map to future performance. When something is not done well, work with the individual to figure out how it should be done next time. (See Chapter 11 on feedback.)

Provide Opportunity. You increase the odds of getting good performance when you provide people the opportunity to fulfill their needs and interests. To use this approach, you must know what members of your work group find interesting, enjoyable, or satisfying. Also, you must have some control over the assignment of work. Then make assignments to those who like to do what needs to be done.

Offer Reward. Another way to gain cooperation and good performance is to offer a reward for what you want done. To be effective, the group member must consider the reward desirable and see there is a good chance of receiving it. Several things can be rewards, such as special privileges, recognition, promotion/reassignment, and pay increases.

67

Threaten Punishment. You can sometimes gain good performance by threatening punishment for poor performance. To be effective, the punishment must be seen as undesirable and enforceable. Do not make idle threats. If good performance does not follow, carry out the punishment in a fair and consistent way. Punishments include reprimands, temporary layoffs, written warnings, and discharge. (When handling the more severe forms of punishment, remember that the employee must be warned and given a reasonable opportunity to improve. See Chapter 17 on discipline.)

Appeal to Values. Sometimes an appeal to a person's values will result in cooperation and good performance. To be effective, you need to know what your work-group members value. Some values that might be appropriate are duty, responsibility, fair play, honesty, obedience (to the law), and pride in high-quality work. Then show the person how doing what you want done is consistent with his or her values.

Personal Request. Often group members will do what you ask simply because you ask. The extent to which this is effective depends upon the importance attached to the relationship and the prospects of the favor being repaid. This approach usually is used to get someone to do something that is considered to be outside the normal duties of the job. For this reason, use it carefully. Do not take advantage of others by making them feel they must do something they would rather not do or risk damaging the relationship by refusing.

CONCLUSION

Some ways to gain cooperation and achieve good performance are more effective than others in the long run. Use your position, knowledge, and relationships within the group to develop and maintain the group's effectiveness. Let people know what you expect of them and give them feedback on how well they do. Then provide as much opportunity as possible for people to do what they find interesting and satisfying. Praise good work. Help those who do not do well learn proper job procedures. Let all members of the group know that their work is important and that they are important people.

Occasionally, individuals may require special attention and other ways of getting cooperation will come into play. You may need to appeal to values, offer rewards, or threaten punishment. None of these approaches is effective over a long time when used with the same person. They are only a means of getting an immediate positive response. Then other forces must take over.

Finally, do not expect miracles. Not everyone will respond. Sometimes, for the benefit of the work group and often the individual involved, the person who is not getting the job done should be discharged. Consider the amount of time and energy you require to work with the person, the impact on the total group, and the prospects for improvement. When you put more into the situation than you gain, you probably will be better off replacing the person.

SUGGESTIONS
- When making job assignments, consider the interests of those available and match the work to employee interests as much as possible.
- Take time to let everyone know how you view their work; provide feedback.
- Be available to contribute your knowledge and experience to helping solve work problems.

12

Providing Feedback

CHAPTER HIGHLIGHTS
- A model for understanding feedback
- A description of three types of feedback
- Guidelines for handling feedback
- A strategy for corrective feedback

People generally need feedback on their performance. They need to know how well they are doing in relation to what is expected. When there are no clear feedback channels, people find their own, such as the grapevine or individual interpretations of things they see happening. For example, people may compare the assignments or promotions they receive to others and conclude they are either doing well or not. Unfortunately, these conclusions may not be accurate because important information may be missing.

Consider the following model. When people act they intend to achieve certain results. Without feedback they never know whether or not they were successful.

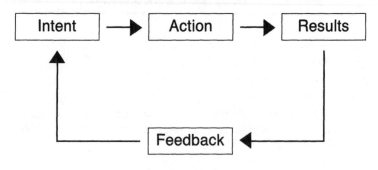

Feedback Model

As supervisor, you are in an excellent position to see that members of your work group receive adequate, appropriate feedback. Rather than ignoring others' needs in this area or leaving them to chance, get actively involved in systematically sharing information with group members. The following ideas will be helpful.

TYPES OF FEEDBACK

There are three types of feedback: informative, reinforcing, and corrective. While all three are intended to increase individual performance, each goes about it in a different way. All three are necessary for an effective work group.

Informative Feedback

Typically, you have access to more information than members of your group. See that key information which you have is provided to members of your group who can use it to improve their output. Such information will let people take informed action rather than operate in the dark. Decisions can then be based on objective data rather than intuition.

Informative feedback is straightforward information. It does not include any judgment of good or bad. Common examples include total production figures for the work group, suggestions from customers for improvements in products or services, number and type of complaints about product or service quality, number of copies made on the office copying machine, and number and type of on-the-job injuries.

With informative feedback, you assume that employees want to do a good job. Therefore, telling them the results of their effort will lead to high future performance. This is undoubtedly true in many cases. However, three other assumptions must also be made:

- If performance is below expectation, they will know why.
- They will know what to do to bring performance in line.
- The circumstances leading to the poor performance are within their control.

Nevertheless, there are situations where these assumptions are inappropriate.

Reinforcing Feedback

Reinforcing feedback has a positive quality factor built in. It is an excellent complement to informative feedback and comes in many forms, including praise, salary increases, promotions, and special privileges. It says to the individual, "You did a good job. Keep up the good work."

The most reliable form of reinforcement is recognition and praise from you. The other forms, while significant, are often beyond your control and occur too infrequently to be truly effective. Do not neglect this area of your responsibilities. Look for opportunities to praise good performance. By doing so, you will be building a road map to the future that will ensure continued high-quality performance. Do not get so caught up in other duties that you fall into the "no news is good news" trap.

Corrective Feedback

From time to time, group members get off the track. The actions taken or results produced do not measure up to expectations. This frequently calls for corrective feedback.

Corrective feedback has a negative quality factor built in. It, too, is an appropriate complement to informative feedback. It says to the individual, "A change is required for the future." This becomes the key to successful corrective feedback. Do not limit your feedback to pointing out mistakes. Take time to provide the necessary guidance and direction to get the person back on track. By doing so, you are adding more details to your road map to the future. Three things are necessary for corrective feedback to be successful:

- The individual must understand what you are saying.
- The individual must accept the information.
- The individual must be able to do something with it.

HANDLING FEEDBACK

Handling feedback successfully requires honesty, skill, courage, and respect for yourself and the other person. This makes it more of a goal to strive for than something you can do immediately. The following guidelines and strategy will help you move toward that goal.

Guidelines for Handling Feedback

To be effective with feedback, you need to minimize the chances for the other person becoming defensive. If this happens, feedback will be rejected. To minimize defensiveness, follow these guidelines.

Be Selective. Reserve feedback for key payoff areas. Do not get a reputation as a nitpicker. Arrange problems in priority and spend your time and energy in those areas that will nurture the important aspects of performance.

Be Specific. Provide precise feedback so the person understands the nature of the feedback and the reason for it. It is much more helpful to tell someone, "Your handling of the customer complaint this morning was well done," than to say, "You have been doing a pretty good job lately." As a general guideline, try to avoid words such as *always* and *never*.

Be Prompt. When your goal is to improve performance, make an effort to reduce the time lag between the performance and the feedback. Time delays may allow mistakes to be repeated. Prompt feedback, on the other hand, capitalizes on the individual's heightened level of interest following the completion of a job.

Be Descriptive. Talk about what you saw or heard rather than conclusions you may have drawn about the person from your observations. Observations are generally accepted as fact, while conclusions are often rejected as incorrect inferences.

Be Sensitive. Sometimes it is appropriate to allow a brief cooling-off period so that you and the other person can engage in a rational discussion. Note whether the other person is very busy or appears emotionally upset. Remember, excellent feedback at the wrong time or place frequently will do more harm than good.

Explore Alternatives. Often what people do appears to them to be the only course of action available at the time. However, this frequently is not the case. The stress of the moment has limited their range of alternatives. Effective feedback will encourage a broader range of vision that includes other alternatives.

Strategy for Corrective Feedback

The following strategy will work for you when you are handling corrective feedback. It is directed to a situation requiring a time period for improvement. Some situations will call for a person to start or stop doing something immediately. These situations should be approached in essentially the same way but obviously do not require an improvement plan.

Get to the Point. Quickly and clearly describe the specific situation or behavior you are concerned about. This is no time for beating around the bush or watering down the feedback just to reduce the chances of potential emotional reactions.

Get a Reaction. After you have described your concern, stop talking and get the other person's reaction. Get him or her talking about the situation under discussion. Expect the individual to be defensive, to rationalize, and to blame others. During this time, convey empathy and understanding for the situation. Do not get caught up in arguing or debating any points raised.

Get Agreement. Get the person to agree with you, at least partially, that the problem or situation cannot be allowed to continue. This may require some selling on your part to convince him or her that whatever you are discussing is in fact inappropriate behavior.

Develop a Plan. Get the other person involved and work together developing a plan for improvement. Do not expect too much. It is better to have a modest plan that will be carried out than a demanding one that will be ignored.

Summarize. Summarize your discussion to ensure understanding. Restate the problem, your expectations for the future, and the plan the two of you have developed to get there.

Follow Up. Set a specific follow-up date to get back together and review progress. Then get together as agreed. At that time, provide appropriate feedback on progress made toward the agreed-upon goal.

CONCLUSION

Everyone needs feedback, i.e., to understand how performance compares to expectations. As supervisor, you must see that the feedback needs of your work group are met.

Providing feedback is very difficult for some supervisors. Corrective feedback is avoided because of potential emotional responses from employees. Reinforcing feedback is avoided so as not to appear soft or insincere. Remember to concentrate your attention on actions or behavior and the impact these have on results. Avoid talking about the person as an individual.

SUGGESTIONS

- Look at the information you receive on your group's performance. How much should be passed on?
- Provide prompt, specific, reinforcing feedback on work well done.
- When giving corrective feedback, always include guidance on how the task should be properly done.
- Do not overload your group with corrective feedback. Focus your time and attention on the areas of greatest payoff.

13
Training Your Staff

CHAPTER HIGHLIGHTS
- An outline for orienting new group members
- Four general learning principles to follow
- How to properly prepare to conduct training
- Four steps for effective instruction

Training is an important responsibility of every supervisor. You may not actually train each member of your group, but you must see that each is trained.

Training responsibilities fall into three categories: orientation to the company and work group for new group members, training in the knowledge and skills required to do the present job successfully, and training in the knowledge and skills required to advance to a higher paying job. Each is important. However, orienting new group members and seeing that all members of the work group know how to do their present job take priority.

ORIENTING NEW GROUP MEMBERS
The first day on the job is an opportunity to set a positive tone and thereby avoid problems that might occur later. The way a person is treated during this period conveys an impression of you and the company. Prepare in advance to make a positive impression.

Key Points to be Covered
To get started right, do not keep a new group member waiting. If you are generally busy at the start of the work day, assign someone else to receive the new person and cover the following points. When your schedule permits, take some time to get acquainted and welcome the newcomer to your group.

Hours of Work. Explain starting and stopping times, how much time is allowed for cleanup at the end of the day, if appropriate, and what the rules are concerning coffee breaks, smoke breaks, and meal periods. If shift work is involved, must a person stay on duty until relieved? What are the rules on required overtime or call-out work? Do days off change from week to week? If so, where and when are schedules posted? Are schedules subject to change after being posted? What are the rules on reporting absences or late arrivals?

Facilities. It is usually most helpful to a new person to have a tour of the work location, at which time the following should be pointed out: washrooms and locker facilities, restrooms, first-aid stations, lunchroom or cafeteria facilities, location of tools and supplies, smoking versus nonsmoking areas, parking areas, and telephones available for personal use.

Rules and Procedures. New people should be given a list of rules and procedures they are expected to follow. Points usually included on such a list are any requirement for wearing identification badges, after-hours signout procedures, restrictions on leaving the department or job site during work hours, and procedures for removing packages from the premises.

Job Assignment. The final orientation step should focus on the new person's work group and job assignment. Some things to cover at this time are the functions of the department, where work comes from and where it goes, quality and quantity standards, safety precautions, and housekeeping requirements.

Introducing the New Group Member

After covering these points, the new member should be introduced to others in the work group and should be assigned to an experienced person to continue the orientation process. The experienced person should be carefully chosen and briefed to ensure that a positive attitude is reflected and that the new member's questions can be answered.

KNOWLEDGE AND SKILLS TRAINING

Knowledge is acquired by reading, listening, and observing. New skills are also learned in several different ways, such as trial and error or copying someone else. However, the most efficient

77

training is accomplished with the help of a good instructor. You can become a good instructor by understanding and being guided by general principles of learning, preparing for the job of instructor, then following a four-step instruction procedure.

General Learning Principles

The following basic principles apply to all learning experiences. When training members of your group, use these principles in the design of the training effort and your expectations of the trainees.

A Skill Must Be Used to Be Remembered. One must continue to do something to remain proficient. Therefore, schedule the training close to the time the knowledge or skills you are teaching will be needed.

Learning Is Based on What Is Already Known. Begin with some assessment of what your trainee knows about what you plan to teach. Because learning can be transferred from one situation to another, during this assessment do not limit yourself to just what is known about the precise operation. For example, if you were teaching someone to operate a forklift, you would want to know any experience your trainee has with forklifts, tractors, cars, or trucks.

Learning Progresses from the Simple to the Complex. When designing training, break the total job down into fairly simple steps. Then progress through each step until the whole job is learned. This provides an opportunity for the trainee to experience success along the way, to remain interested, and to be motivated to learn the whole operation. When you do not break the job down, you run the risk of overwhelming and thereby frustrating the trainee.

Everyone Is Different. Some people learn quickly; others take longer. Learning does not progress at a steady rate even for the fast learner. There will be breakthroughs where understanding is achieved, but there will also be times when seemingly no progress is made. Repetition is required to master almost any task. Do not expect anyone to learn something with just one demonstration.

Preparing to Teach

Good instructors are prepared. Most instructors have experience in the operations they teach; therefore, they know their material. However, more than that is required. Other items to prepare include procedures to be sure that nothing is left out and support material or training aids to illustrate and clarify the material being taught.

The Job Training Breakdown. When an experienced person teaches job details, significant points may be left out. Assumptions are made that "everyone knows that," or some detail is so routine that it is overlooked during the training period. To overcome these potential problems, prepare a job breakdown. (See example.)

JOB TRAINING BREAKDOWN

Important Steps	Key Points
(What the worker must do to cause the job to advance to the next step.)	(What the worker must know to do the step correctly, safely, and efficiently.)
1. _____	1. _____
2. _____	2. _____
3. _____	3. _____

In completing a job breakdown, think through and record each step required to complete a job. Do not assume anything. Under key points, list the information required to do each step properly: where something is located, how to position something, or safety precautions to prevent injury. (Practice this analysis with a simple task, such as refilling a stapler.)

Training Aids. Training is much easier when oral instructions are supplemented with appropriate training aids. Consider these possibilities: training manuals, films, or videotapes that describe the job and show what is to be done. Trainees can study these in advance and can be prepared to move ahead more quickly in learning the details of the job. Other training aids that are helpful include pieces of machinery to be operated or repaired that trainees can practice on before actually taking over a job, photographs or slides of products to be produced or equipment to be operated or maintained, samples of products or forms to be completed, and flow diagrams showing where things come from, what is done to them, and where they go.

How to Instruct

With a job breakdown completed and training aids prepared, you are ready to begin instructing. Using the learning principles discussed earlier, the following four-step process will lead to effective and efficient results.

Step 1—Prepare the Trainee. During this step, develop interest in learning by pointing out the value of being able to perform the task. Also find out what the trainee knows about the task from prior experience so you do not duplicate anything.

Step 2—Present the Operation. Tell, show, and illustrate the operation, one step at a time. As you present each step, stress each key point associated with that step.

Step 3—Involve the Trainee. Have the trainee perform each step in the operation and explain the key points. Correct any errors you observe and continue the process until you are satisfied the trainee knows the operation. This step must not be omitted. Both demonstration and practice must be provided to verify understanding.

Step 4—Follow Up. When you are satisfied with what you see, turn the operation over to the trainee. Check back frequently to answer questions, correct errors, and praise accomplishments. Taper off this coaching activity as the trainee's ability to handle the operation is verified.

CONCLUSION

Too often, training is handled in a haphazard way. New group members are either assumed to know how to do the work or are left on their own to learn by trial and error. This does not provide for a knowledgeable, skilled work group. Alternatively, supervisors should pick up their responsibilities to see that training is well planned and carried out.

The purpose of training should always be to improve individual performance and thereby improve total work-group performance. This can be achieved through increased knowledge or improved skills. Telling someone something will increase knowledge; however, it will not improve skills. Skills are improved through practice. Therefore, training must be designed to allow hands-on experience in order to bridge the gap between knowing how to do something and actually being able to do it.

SUGGESTIONS
- Establish a procedure for receiving new members into your work group.
- With the help of each group member, develop job procedure guides that describe what is to be done and how to do it.
- Develop job breakdowns on the jobs in your area for which people are frequently being trained.

14

Evaluating Performance

CHAPTER HIGHLIGHTS
- Four reasons for evaluating performance
- How to evaluate performance
- What to evaluate
- Three pitfalls to avoid

Performance evaluation is an ongoing responsibility of every supervisor. As you consider how well members of your group are doing their jobs, you are evaluating their performance. When you decide whom to recommend for promotion, transfer, reassignment, salary increase, or termination, you are evaluating performance.

To handle this part of your job successfully, several ideas need to be considered. First, understand why you are investing time and effort in this activity. Then look at the process itself, how it is carried out and potential pitfalls to avoid.

REASONS FOR EVALUATING PERFORMANCE

Performance evaluation prepares you for other responsibilities. It is never an end in itself. It is homework to be done so you can hold meaningful feedback discussions, make appropriate administrative recommendations, and determine where performance improvement is required. It also provides a written record to substantiate actions that differentiate among group members. Therefore, it serves a dual function: an employee feedback system and a management information system.

Feedback to Employees

Nearly everyone is interested in how his or her performance is viewed by management. In the absence of specific feedback, people often form their own conclusions by comparing their experiences with others around them. This sometimes leads to wrong conclusions. To be sure members of your group clearly understand how their performance is viewed, give specific feedback. It is a powerfully motivating force for future performance. Such feedback can only be given after careful evaluation.

Administrative Decisions

As a supervisor, you are expected to make recommendations on various administrative decisions affecting members of your group. These decisions include whether to continue someone's employment, who should be promoted, if someone should be given a salary increase, and who should be transferred or reassigned. At least a portion of the input to all of these decisions is an evaluation of an individual's present level of performance.

Performance Improvement Planning

Occasionally, a person's performance does not measure up to expectations. Improvement is needed. These decisions are based on performance evaluation. Also, performance evaluation provides the diagnostic work necessary to determine the root cause of poor performance, thus pointing out where to concentrate improvement efforts.

Documentation

More and more today, the various administrative decisions made by management are being subjected to review by outside parties. Depending upon individual circumstances, these might be a labor arbitrator, an EEOC investigator, or a civil court judge. To verify the appropriateness of decisions made, management must provide evidence for review. Performance evaluation records serve as excellent evidence when a sound system is administered equitably.

THE EVALUATION PROCESS

Most people do a good job. Some, particularly new group members, do not measure up fully and therefore need special attention. Others exceed expectations and therefore become candidates

83

for special opportunities. You need to identify those members of your group who fall into these three basic categories. The following suggestions will help you accomplish the task equitably.

How to Evaluate

Any evaluative decision is made by comparison. Whatever is being evaluated is compared to something else, and it either exceeds, equals, or falls short in the comparison. One of the most important aspects of performance evaluation is to use an equitable base of comparison and apply it consistently when evaluating the peformance of different group members or the same member at different times.

Performance expectations alleviate potential problems in choosing a base of comparison. It is fairly easy to determine that employees either exceed, equal, or fall short of their agreed-upon expectations.

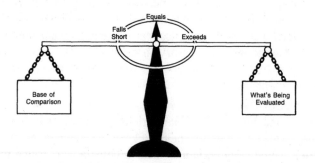

The Evaluation Process

From this basic decision, you may bring other comparison bases into consideration for unique purposes. For example, you might compare performance in a current time period with performance in a prior time period when counseling a group member. Or you might compare one individual to another to decide who would be better for a particular job assignment.

What to Evaluate

Performance evaluation should concentrate on results achieved. That is why the person is on the payroll. In most cases, results are clearly observable and therefore are readily measurable. Generally, results can be measured from four perspectives:

- Quantity—How much was accomplished? How does that compare to what was expected? Did any circumstances beyond the individual's control affect the amount of results achieved, either positively or negatively?
- Quality—How good were the results? How does actual work done compare to the quality expected? What relationship exists between quality and quantity? For example, some people spend so much time trying to attain perfection that volume of output suffers, while others—in order to meet volume standards—let quality slip.
- Cost—What costs were incurred in the process of achieving results? Consider such things as materials, tools, and services. How do costs compare to budget?
- Timeliness—Is work completed on time? If not, why not? Are delays due to circumstances beyond the individual's control, or are they due to poor planning and control?

As a diagnostic tool to aid in determining the root causes of poor performance, you should evaluate work habits. This category might include attendance, punctuality, housekeeping, safety practices, planning, and organization.

Finally, performance evaluation may consider qualities observable in a person's present assignment, which in turn are significant in a future promotional opportunity. The elements of the future job that can actually be observed in the present assignment must be identified. This typically includes certain demonstrated administrative, technical, and interpersonal skills.

Potential Pitfalls

Performance evaluation is subject to many potential pitfalls. If not avoided, these pitfalls lead to inaccurate, unfair evaluations from which improper action may flow.

Rateability. Some supervisors attempt to evaluate things that are essentially unratable. Stick with what you can see, hear, or touch. Avoid trying to evaluate something that is inferred. You can compare actual results against expected results and form a sound conclusion. However, evaluations of issues such as interest

85

in the job, loyalty, and attitude are based on inferences drawn from other observed behavior.

Consider the following model. Only actions and results are observable. Other issues are inferred.

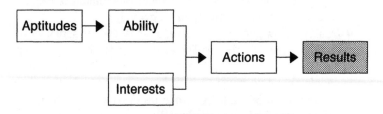

Elements Contributing to Results

Relevancy. Evaluations that omit essentials or give undue weight to trivia are irrelevant. Specific pitfalls to watch for include being influenced by things that have no specific bearing on performance such as physical appearance or congeniality, letting one episode of good or bad performance disproportionately affect the evaluation of a total period, and over-looking (and therefore not considering) important areas of an individual's total responsibilities.

Variability. Supervisors sometimes do not reflect differences in performance among members of their work group. Where an adequate sampling exists, a range of performance can be expected. When it does not occur, the supervisor may be too lenient, evaluating all performance as adequate or better, or failing to distinguish performance levels by evaluating all performance as adequate without any high or low evaluations.

Individual Bias. Occasionally, evaluations of performance may be influenced by a supervisor's biases. This results in an evaluation that does not reflect the true level of performance; it is either too high or too low. Individual bias can be minimized by involving others in the evaluation process who have a direct knowledge of the person's performance level. This could include having all evaluations reviewed by the next level of management or having other supervisors participate in the evaluation process.

CONCLUSION

A sound performance evaluation system draws on both supervisor and group member. Together you negotiate performance expectations for the future. With expectations set, the next step is to monitor progress. There is a wide range in your level of involvement in this step. Some group members may need to be monitored closely and frequently. Others, based on your experience with them, may need only occasional contact. However, do not totally neglect this area of responsibility. Supervisors have a right and a need to know what progress is being made toward expected results.

Finally, using information obtained through monitoring progress, evaluate the results. The evaluation of performance prepares you to give feedback, make recommendations on administrative decisions, and provide appropriate counsel on performance improvement. It is never an end in itself. The performance evaluation system also provides documentation to substantiate administrative decisions.

Evaluations should reflect a true picture of a person's contribution. There are several pitfalls to avoid in order to accomplish this. Consider all relevant issues that can be observed. Be willing to distinguish among levels of performance, and avoid personal bias and extraneous issues in the process. Make a simple comparison of what was actually accomplished to what was expected for the period.

SUGGESTIONS

- Develop performance expectations for each member of your group.
- Formally evaluate the performance of each member of your group once a year.
- Clearly define the base of comparison you use in the evaluation process.
- Avoid the pitfalls discussed.

15

Reviewing Performance

CHAPTER HIGHLIGHTS
- How to prepare for a meaningful review discussion
- Specific guidance on opening, developing and closing a discussion
- Three things to do following the discussion

Many organizations have policies requiring supervisors to conduct periodic performance discussions with members of their work group. Even if your organization does not have such a policy, you may decide it is appropriate. Such discussions allow you to talk with your group members about where you have been during the past year, to put the total year in perspective, and to see where you are going during the coming year. These discussions help people answer questions like: How am I doing? Where can I go from here? and How do I get there?

To guarantee success, consider these ideas before, during, and after the discussion.

BEFORE THE DISCUSSION

Advance preparation is crucial to the success of a performance discussion. This phase should begin as much as a month prior to the actual meeting.

The first step is to update yourself on the individual's performance history. This includes reviewing available records and gathering additional data you may need from other records or from other appropriate people. With a data base established, decide on the major emphasis of your discussion. Think through potential trouble spots and make a brief outline of items you want to cover.

The next step in your preparation is to arrange for the meeting. Start by selecting a private place. These meetings should not

88

be interrupted nor overheard. Then make an appointment, stating the purpose of the meeting. When making the appointment, be considerate of demands the other person may be facing. Select a time when you can expect his or her undivided attention.

HOLDING THE DISCUSSION

The spirit that should characterize the discussion is one of working together—a collaborative problem-solving approach. To help achieve that spirit, consider three distinct phases of the discussion and the part you should play in each.

Opening the Discussion

During this phase you set the stage for what follows. Begin by putting the other person at ease. To do this, start with a friendly greeting and engage in general but related conversation. For example, you might talk about the general practice in your department of holding this type of discussion and the benefits one can expect as an outcome.

While you are talking in this general way, observe the other person for signs of stress. These signs might be tense and rigid posture, limited responses to questions, or a higher-pitched voice. Continue the general discussion until these signs subside, then move on to setting the specific topic for the day's discussion, the amount of time you have available for it, and the part you expect the other person to play.

Developing the Discussion

As you develop the discussion, involve your group member by asking about reactions to your ideas so you can draw out his or her opinions. During this phase the portion of the time each of you talk should be about equal. When the other person is talking, listen attentively and make notes if necessary.

How to Involve the Other Person. There are several ways for you to involve the other person and thereby maintain the balance in the discussion. Use these ideas as they seem appropriate.

- Display a supportive attitude.
- Control your emotions.

- Encourage continued conversation.
- Use silence appropriately.
- Restate the other's opinions, attitudes, and feelings to encourage elaboration.
- Ask questions.

Questioning Techniques. Some questions encourage discussion while others limit it. Learn to state your questions to help the other person think and go into some detail with the answer. Generally avoid those questions that can be answered yes or no. Above all, listen to the answers and be careful about forming conclusions on too little data. Some questions that may prove useful are:

- What parts of your job do you enjoy most? Why?
- What parts of your job do you find difficult? Why?
- What can I do to make things better for you?
- How do you feel about your prospects with this company?
- What can you do to improve your value to the company?
- What are your immediate goals?
- What are your long-range goals?
- What do you see yourself doing five years from now?
- What do you see as your major strengths?
- What is your understanding of your duties and responsibilities? Priorities? Schedules? Standards? Expected results?
- What things would you like to talk about?

Needless to say, a discussion cannot be conducted just as a series of questions. It will be appropriate for you to add your thoughts on the various topics as they are discussed. This will either be a confirmation of the other person's view or a clarification where you see things differently.

Finally, ask only one question at a time. Some people have a habit of asking three or four questions, leaving the other person confused over which one to answer. Once you ask a question, do not jump in and answer it. Provide the other person ample time to consider the issue and reply.

Closing the Discussion

Review your outline. When you have covered all of the points you planned to discuss as well as those introduced by your group member, close the discussion.

You need to address two important issues in the closing: summarize the key points and check the other person's understanding. The best way to do this is to ask him or her to summarize. Then you can check to see that the two of you agree. The more common way of having the supervisor do the summarizing does not reflect the other person's understanding.

FOLLOWING THE DISCUSSION

Following the discussion, you have responsibilities to complete before you are finished. These include the following.

Summarize for the Record

Write a brief summary of the discussion. This should include key points discussed, reactions, and plans or action items agreed to. Some supervisors ask the group member to read and edit a draft of the summary to be sure they are in agreement. Others actually have the group member write the summary. Consider what would be best for you, recognizing that if you talked about it, both of you should agree that it was said.

Complete the Administrative Details

If your organization has a formal performance review procedure, there probably are forms to complete and submit to your supervisor or to the personnel office. Handle these details promptly. The longer you delay, the larger the backlog of work and the greater the chance that you may not remember the details of the discussion.

Follow Through on Commitments

If you agreed to do anything during the course of the discussion, follow through. A simple request for information that is set aside and then forgotten can have serious impact on a person's attitude. It indicates that you are not interested—that you do not care.

CONCLUSION

A good discussion is a two-way conversation spotlighting on-the-job issues. Its aims are mutual to supervisor and work group members. Each needs the other to have a satisfactory work experience. The discussion's main orientation should be to the future. Obviously, a review of past performance looks to the past, but that review of the past must be projected into the future with encouragement to maintain present performance or to improve.

Several procedures and techniques to accomplish a good discussion exist. However, no technique can be more valuable than the simple notion of respect for the person with whom you are talking. If you are sensitive to his or her interests and needs, you can accomplish a lot. Most members of your group need to maintain their personal dignity and feel your support for the effort they put forth on the job.

SUGGESTIONS

- Give members of your group an opportunity at least annually to discuss their performance.
- Be sure to let the other person know what you want to discuss and why.
- Set a time that is convenient for both of you.
- Ensure a private place for the discussion.
- Encourage a two-way discussion by maintaining a friendly, receptive attitude.

16
Handling Performance Improvement

CHAPTER HIGHLIGHTS
- Performance defined
- The three variables in the performance equation with suggestions for improving each one
- How to use a collaborative goal setting strategy

As a result of performance evaluation and review, it may be evident that some members of your group need to improve their performance. When this is the case, the three-part strategy presented here will increase your odds of success.

PERFORMANCE DEFINED

The best place to begin is to define performance. Here, it is considered to be the results of a person's efforts. This is what you, as supervisor, are concerned about. As discussed in Chapter 14, performance looks at results along four dimensions:

- Quantity—How much was accomplished? How does that compare to what was expected? Did any circumstances beyond the individual's control affect the amount of results achieved, either positively or negatively?
- Quality—How good were the results? How does actual work done compare to the quality expected? What relationship exists between the quality and quantity? For example, some people spend so much time trying to attain perfection that volume of output suffers; others let quality slip in order to meet volume standards.
- Cost—What costs were incurred in the process of achieving results? Consider such things as materials, tools, and services. How do costs compare to budget?

- Timeliness—Is work completed on time? If not, why not? Are delays due to circumstances beyond the individual's control or are they due to poor planning and control?

When there is a deficiency in any of these four areas, an improvement in performance is needed.

THE PERFORMANCE EQUATION

Performance is a function of three variables:
- *The Person*—talents, skills, interests, values, and motives.
- *The Job*—the work assigned and the opportunity it provides for achievement, growth, recognition, and advancement.
- *The Situation*—organization, administrative constraints, climate, supervision, and resources assigned.

When addressing performance improvement, examine each of these variables in detail. A change in any one may have a significant impact on overall results. Your responsibility is to assure a favorable interaction and balance among the three.

The Person

This may be the most difficult factor in the equation to influence. Therefore, a positive approach is generally most productive. With this in mind, performance improvement efforts should meet four criteria.

Build on Strengths. Performance improvement should focus on strengths, not weaknesses. Chances of success are greater when using or developing existing talents rather than trying to develop new or deficient ones.

Build on Likes. There is a significant relationship between what people like to do and what they do well. Therefore, expressed likes are a sound source for development and growth.

Consider Career Interests. Performance improvement should be compatible with career interests. When someone has strong career interests, capitalize on them. A recognizable relationship between career objectives and improvement activities will increase a person's motivation to achieve the desired improvement.

Be Short Ranged. Goals and ambitions change as people are exposed to new experiences. Therefore, performance improvement should be short ranged in order to remain flexible. Being short ranged also provides more frequent satisfaction and motivation from accomplishing desired results.

The Job

The work itself may provide opportunities for increasing individual effectiveness and providing growth opportunities. To build improvement and growth potential into a job, consider the following opportunities.

Look At Job Design. Should work be reassigned within a section or department to provide opportunity for improved performance? Consider the talents and interests in your group and the work to be done. Then work out the best possible match between the two. Also delegate as much authority and responsibility as each one can handle.

Provide Special Assignments. Provide opportunity to serve on special assignments, task forces, study teams, and committees.

Consider Job Rotation. If promotion is impossible, a rotation of assignments may provide needed challenge for continued growth. Job rotation, however, should be long enough to provide a representative sample of work and to require people to live with the results of some of their decisions. It should fill developmental needs of those involved, and the standards of performance should be at a challenging level.

The Situation

When focusing on the work situation, a number of areas become opportunities for improvement.

Consider Organizational Structure. Are there reporting relationships that need improving? Is one area or subunit ineffective? Are there too many or too few levels of supervision? How can people and their work be better organized? These offer opportunity to improve results and provide growth.

What About Resources? Each group member is allocated certain resources, including money, space, facilities, tools, and equipment. All of these need to be reviewed to see that they are adequate and in line with the priority of the work.

Analyze Work Schedules. Work schedules can be controlled or changed to facilitate getting the work done. By reviewing progress against schedules and considering business needs and individual work habits, it may become apparent that a schedule change is in order. Scheduling draws on a person's talents in the areas of planning, coordinating, and allocating resources.

Look At Your Style. Your style of supervising is probably the most important factor in the work situation. It includes a variety of things you do in the day-to-day operation of your department, such as how you delegate, how you follow up on work assignments, how you communicate, the standards you set, the methods you endorse, your system of rewards and recognition, and the extent to which you encourage members of your group to take risks. Your behavior in each of these areas affects individual growth.

GOAL SETTING

Performance improvement does not just happen. Direction and motivation are necessary for it to occur. An effective way of obtaining direction and motivation is to use the goal-setting approach.

Identify Improvement Goal

Start with an idea of what you are trying to accomplish—a goal to be reached. The improvement goal is not a production goal. Rather, it is a goal to remove some obstacle that is preventing the production level you seek. Performance improvement goals are the result of an analysis of all elements in the performance equation. Examples of performance improvement goals are to increase the level of knowledge, to organize a work area better, to improve working relationships with another department, and to balance work demands over the entire month.

Develop A Plan

Many supervisors stop with the improvement goal. As a result, group members often complain that their shortcomings are pointed out to them but no help is provided in overcoming them. This problem can be alleviated by working with the individual and developing a plan for achieving the goal. What needs to be done and in what sequence?

Identify Information Sources

What does the person need to know in order to carry out the plan, and where can necessary information be obtained? Often, people are left on their own to find necessary information. It is generally more effective to discuss the point and share your experience.

Set a Time Schedule

Lay out a reasonable time period for achieving the improvement plan. Also schedule appropriate follow-up discussions keyed to steps in the plan. Target dates and follow-up talks contribute substantially to achieving a goal. Almost everyone is more inclined to do something when there is a date set for reviewing progress. Without a follow-up discussion, things tend to be put off until later.

COLLABORATION

When more than one person is involved in doing something, three choices are available for handling the situation: directive, collaborative, and delegative. These choices are a function of a supervisor's willingness to allow group members to have a say in what happens.

DEGREES OF INVOLVEMENT

	Directive	Collaborative									Delegative
Supervisor	100%	90	80	70	60	50	40	30	20	10	0
Group member	0	10	20	30	40	50	60	70	80	90	100%

Two relevant correlations exist with the degree of involvement. One correlation shows that as an individual's influence in the decision increases, satisfaction with the decision increases. The optimum point of satisfaction for both supervisor and group

97

member exists at the 60–40 or 50–50 degrees of involvement. The other correlation shows that as an individual's influence in the decision increases, his or her sense of responsibility to carry out the decision increases to a point and then begins to decrease. The maximum point of responsibility for both supervisor and group member is at the 50–50 degree of involvement.

These observations clearly establish that the ideal approach to performance improvement is to involve the other person in examining all of the elements of the performance equation and developing a plan for improvement. You are an active part of the discussion, but you are not directing the outcome.

CONCLUSION

Performance improvement is an area of responsibility for each supervisor. However, it does not just happen. An effective means of accomplishing improvement includes considering all factors influencing performance in a collaborative discussion with the group member involved. Through the discussion, you can establish improvement goals and develop a strategy and schedule for attaining them.

SUGGESTIONS
- Extend your range of examination in determining the causes of poor performance.
- Involve the other person in the process.
- Set improvement goals with specific plans and follow-up discussions.

17

Handling Discipline

CHAPTER HIGHLIGHTS
- Eight types of discipline to consider
- Seven guidelines for achieving a positive response to discipline
- Five key steps to ensure fair treatment

Occasionally, someone in your work group will do something that will require you to take disciplinary action. It might be substandard job performance, too many absences, outright violation of an order, rule, or procedure, or some illegal act such as stealing, fighting, gambling, or dealing in drugs.

Facing these kinds of issues and handling them in a way that has a positive effect on work-group performance is a real challenge. A few guidelines can help you handle this part of your job effectively.

TYPES OF DISCIPLINARY ACTION

Discipline embraces all of the action you take to mold the behavior of your group. It is not necessarily punishment. Many different types of action are available to you. The appropriate action depends upon the facts in each case.

Feedback. Simply letting members of your group know how you view their performance can have a very positive effect on the group. Many people are willing to make an adjustment in their performance when their shortcomings are brought to their attention.

Coaching. Most supervisors do not think of coaching as a disciplinary action. However, its purpose is to improve performance. Therefore, it should not be overlooked. When substandard performance appears to be due to lack of job knowledge or skills,

99

coaching could be appropriate. Work with the person to teach, guide, and encourage.

Oral Reprimand. When someone should make an immediate change in the way something is done, an oral reprimand may be in order. When handling an oral reprimand, be clear and specific about what is to be stopped or started. Do not argue or debate side issues, and do not talk about the person in a demeaning or derogatory way.

Written Reprimand. Sometimes it is appropriate to put a reprimand in writing. This typically has more impact than an oral reprimand. It is used with more severe problems or after an oral reprimand has not resulted in the necessary improvement.

Probation. When on probation an individual has a specified time deadline by which to show improvement or be terminated. Probation usually is handled in writing in order to have a record on which to base the termination if improvement does not occur. It is most commonly used for poor work practices, including absenteeism and excessive tardiness.

Temporary Layoff. Violations of rules and minor illegal acts often are treated with a temporary layoff or suspension. The time off varies from one day to six weeks, according to the severity of the situation. In most cases, layoffs are without pay and therefore amount to a monetary fine. The details of the problem and the length of the suspension usually are written and given to the individual involved.

Demotion. When someone cannot handle the duties of a job assignment adequately, demotion can be appropriate. Demotion should not be used as punishment for non-job-related activities.

Termination. When it appears that there is little chance of bringing someone's performance up to an acceptable level, termination may be the best course of action. Also, some acts are so severe (such as major theft) that termination is appropriate as an example to others who may be tempted to do something similar. This category also includes requested resignations. When it appears that a person's interests are not being met on a job, it may be appropriate to request him or her to seek employment elsewhere.

GENERAL GUIDELINES

When handling discipline, a positive reaction from the group member involved is necessary to reach the goal of improved performance. Sometimes other reactions are experienced. For example, rather than being motivated to improve performance, someone may be motivated to retaliate or get even. The following guidelines will help you experience a positive reaction.

Be Sure of the Facts. Before taking any disciplinary action, dig as deeply as necessary to get all of the facts. What happened? What was this person's part in it?

Listen. Give the individual involved ample opportunity to explain what happened and why. Do not go into the investigation with your mind made up about what you are going to do.

Control Your Feelings. Stay calm. Do not do something that will only create new problems, such as name calling.

Avoid Entrapment. Do not set out to get someone. Unless you have sufficient information to suggest that something wrong is taking place, do not get involved. To do otherwise only breeds distrust in the equity and justice of the system.

Keep Records. Make notes on what happened and what you did about it. Records may be important later to demonstrate fair and equitable treatment. On the other hand, set a time limit for keeping records. For example, it would be reasonable to destroy records of disciplinary action after two years of good performance.

Know Your Authority. What action can you take without checking with anyone? What can you only recommend to higher authority? Can you send someone home, with or without pay, while an investigation is carried out? Know your authority and operate within it.

Keep Others Advised. In most companies, there are other people you should keep advised when you are working with a discipline problem. This typically includes your boss and whoever handles personnel. It might include an equal opportunity officer and a labor attorney.

ENSURING FAIR TREATMENT

In general, five criteria are used to evaluate whether discipline has been handled fairly. These criteria have been established over the years by labor arbitrators in discipline cases. They are appropriate whether or not you have a labor contract.

Warn in Advance. A person must be advised of rules and the penalties for their violation. This can be handled orally or in writing. Some conduct, however, can be reasonably expected to be generally known as unacceptable, such as major theft or coming to work drunk.

Relate Rules and Orders to the Business. Rules and orders can be enforced that contribute to the orderly, efficient, safe operation of the business. Additionally, the rules and orders must not require unreasonable performance, such as jeopardizing a person's safety or violating one's integrity.

Investigate the Facts. Before disciplinary action is taken, make an effort to learn whether the person actually disobeyed a rule or order and whether there were any possible justifications for a violation. The investigation must be conducted fairly and objectively. This means locating witnesses and evidence, not just operating on the basis of voluntary information.

Be Equitable. Rules, orders, and penalties must be applied without discrimination. If you have been lax in enforcing a rule, you can overcome this by telling everyone that you intend to start enforcing it from this point forward.

Match the Discipline to the Offense. A trivial violation does not justify harsh and unreasonable discipline. However, a person's prior record must be considered. A series of minor offenses may accumulate and justify discipline that the last act alone would not justify. On the other hand, a long history of good performance may justify less severe treatment in a given situation.

CONCLUSION

Discipline is something to use to help correct behavior that interferes with the work group achieving its purpose in an orderly manner. It is a rational action taken by you—not an emotional reaction.

When working with a discipline problem, use the idea of progressive discipline. It is based on the principle that a person is entitled to an opportunity to improve. At the same time, he or she is entitled to an explicit warning of the consequences of not improving. The normal steps in the progression are:

- Feedback
- Oral reprimand
- Written reprimand
- Probation
- Termination

A person may change before you get to the termination step. However, if change does not occur, a clear record of adequate warning can be demonstrated.

When handling discipline, nothing can take the place of good judgment. Be objective in viewing the facts, including any extenuating circumstances. Then exercise judgment in your final decision. Keep your goal in mind and take the action that helps you achieve the goal. There is no need to belittle, embarrass, or intimidate anyone.

SUGGESTIONS
- Know the limits of your authority.
- Learn how other supervisors have handled similar situations.
- Be consistent yet equitable in handling discipline.
- Keep good notes on every disciplinary case.

18

Handling Terminations

CHAPTER HIGHLIGHTS
- The supervisor's obligations for maintaining work group quality
- The three steps in a termination decision
- How to tell a group member he or she is terminated

Terminating the services of a member of your group is probably the most difficult task you will face as a supervisor. Many supervisors avoid these duties because of fears of what might happen—both during the discussion and following it. These fears frequently can be overcome by recognizing your obligations to your work group, your responsibilities to the individual, and developing an approach to handling the discussion that ensures success.

Often, obligations to the group are not considered. As supervisor, you have a duty to see that members of your group are capable and willing to do their share of the work. When this is not the case, others have to do more in order to get the job done. When someone is not measuring up, everyone knows it. Your failure to take appropriate action is obvious; as a result, you may be seen as a weak supervisor.

In addition to the work group, you also have responsibilities to the inadequate performer. People frequently get caught up in unproductive relationships. It often is better to end these relationships and move on to new ones that have a better chance of success. By terminating an inadequate performer, you can encourage the person to seek opportunity that more closely matches his or her skills and interests. In the long run, this is certainly more desirable than drifting along, never doing well and never enjoying any success on the job until age makes it difficult to find new employment. More often than not, those who are terminated go on to quite satisfying careers in other lines of work for which they are better suited.

To experience these positive outcomes, you must handle the termination properly. The following ideas will help you see that all of the appropriate details are covered.

THE TERMINATION DECISION

The importance of the termination decision is so significant it must be handled with both fairness and objectivity. Preparation leading up to it should focus on proper evaluation of the person's performance, a probationary period for improvement, and an objective third party review of the final decision.

Performance Evaluation

Some terminations are based on nonperformance-related activities such as theft of company property, fighting, and bringing weapons or illicit drugs to the job site. Terminations for these reasons need not be substantiated by performance evaluation. (See Chapter 17 on discipline.)

Terminations for inadequate performance, on the other hand, must be supported by evaluation. This isolates areas of performance where improvement is required and provides evidence to outside agencies that the termination was handled fairly. (See Chapter 14 on performance evaluation.)

For evaluation to be an effective tool, you must be completely honest with group members about the quality of their work. Otherwise, you may find good performers are frustrated at having their performance evaluated the same as poor performers. When you have to take further action against poor performers, you will not be able to support your actions with documentary evidence.

When poor performance has been determined, take corrective action. Do not continue to reward marginal or inadequate performance with salary increases or other types of rewards. When you do so, the individual will assume there is no problem. Further, counsel the person around areas of needed improvement. (See Chapter 16 on handling performance problems.) If an

105

immediate improvement is not experienced, place the poor performer on notice.

Probation

Placing a group member on probation or notice clarifies the gravity of the situation. It clearly points out that the individual's job is in jeopardy and specifies a time period for improvement. The time period may vary from a week to a month, depending upon the nature of improvement required.

Many times, poor performers will make the desired change in performance and will become contributing members of the work group. Other times, they will seemingly ignore the need for change and continue as though nothing were said. Each of these alternatives is easy to deal with. Where improvement is achieved, compliment the individual, remove the probationary notice, and proceed as with other group members. Where no effort is made to improve, continue with steps to remove the person from the work group.

The difficult case is the one who makes some effort but does not achieve the desired level of performance. There is a tendency to be lenient—to give the person another chance. Equity suggests that you be open to circumstances. Why was the desired performance level not achieved? How much progress was made? Taking factors such as these into consideration may occasionally justify an extension of probation. However, be careful about accepting excuses. If the terms of the probation were reasonable, failure to fulfill them is sufficient reason for termination. Otherwise you may have a member of your group who continually will do just enough to get by and will have plenty of excuses to support his or her lack of accomplishment.

Third Party Review

To verify fairness and objectivity, every proposed termination should be reviewed by someone else prior to the decision being considered final. Typically, this review is handled by your immediate supervisor or your personnel officer. The review should consider the issues of fairness, equity, and objectivity. Therefore, you should be sure your proposal can pass these tests.

Fairness. Has this person been expected to do something others are not expected to do? Has the individual been discriminated against? You should not terminate someone for either doing or not doing something when others are not treated the same in response to similar actions. For example, even though a member of your work group has a very poor attendance record, it is not fair to terminate that person if others have equal or worse records and are not treated similarly.

Equity. Does the group member's behavior or lack of performance justify termination, or have you overreacted? There are no ironclad guidelines of what constitutes equitable treatment. However, you can look at company history to see how others have been treated under similar circumstances. Also, you can look at what is generally accepted as appropriate or inappropriate work-place behavior.

Objectivity. Is your decision based on facts, or are you letting your emotions rule your actions? This point requires you to have records to verify what has occurred, including dates of discussions and terms of probation. Records are particularly important when a termination decision is challenged. If you must justify your decision to an arbitrator, judge, or EEOC investigator, you will need records to prove your objectivity.

THE TERMINATION NOTIFICATION

The emotional impact of being terminated varies greatly among individuals. Some people are relieved that an undesirable situation is finally resolved. Others experience shock, depression, anger, self-pity, confusion, or loss of self-confidence. There may be anxiety about finding another job. There may be concern about the reaction of family and friends. There may be financial difficulties to handle. For some people the experience of termination is as severe as divorce. Anything you can do to minimize the impact on the individual will be helpful.

Principles

To help minimize the impact of the experience, keep the following three principles in mind.

Dignity. Everyone is entitled to dignity. There is nothing to be gained and much to be lost by belittling or berating someone in the process of termination. Do not blame or accuse. What was done is history, and the natural consequences of that history are now being played out. Help the person save face as much as possible.

Understanding. Do not try to depersonalize the experience. Be sensitive to the individual's reactions and try to understand the feelings being experienced. Remember that reactions vary, so stay in tune with this person as an individual. Try to understand and respond accordingly.

Positive Outlook. Focus attention on the positive aspects of the experience. Point out, as appropriate, that the person can now find a job that more closely matches his or her skills and interests. Look at this experience as a learning opportunity. How can the problems experienced here be avoided in future employment? This is an opportunity to get a fresh start. How can you make the best of it? Rather than seeing it as an ending experience, look at it as a new beginning—starting over with a clean slate.

Preparing for the Discussion

The decision to terminate has been made. Now the only step remaining is to advise the individual of the decision. Two sets of information need to be pulled together as you prepare for the discussion. First, make a final review of your records so you are completely familiar with all of the details of the case. Second, check with the appropriate authority—usually your personnel officer—about termination policy and benefits. Is it appropriate to terminate the person immediately and then provide a week or two of additional pay in lieu of notice? How will the final paycheck be handled? How will benefits such as savings plan settlements and insurance plan conversions be handled? Will the group member receive pay in lieu of earned vacation credits? Is there outplacement counseling available? Having completed your homework, it is time to hold the discussion.

Holding the Dicussion

There is no absolute right way to conduct a termination discussion. However, there are some guidelines that increase the odds of success.

Timing. Do not ruin special occasions by terminating someone immediately prior to holidays, birthdays, or wedding anniversaries. Beyond selecting the best day, also consider the appropriate time during the day. If the person is not expected to return to work, hold the discussion late in the day. This provides two benefits: the individual will not have to explain leaving early and others will not be available to hear about the experience. On the other hand, if the person is expected to work a few more days, hold the discussion early in the day. The individual will be able to deal with the news better and can move in a positive direction following the discussion.

Setting. The discussion should be held in your office with you seated behind your desk. This allows for the privacy to which the situation is entitled. It also adds formality and authority to your position.

Approach. Be straightforward and direct. Get to the point immediately. Remember, this probably is not the first time you have talked about the problem. State the reason for the termination, point out that the decision has been reviewed and confirmed by others, then stop and wait for a reaction before going further. Consider something like, "We have talked about your performance record several times. You have been on notice for the past two weeks and, unfortunately, you have not been able to bring your performance up to the specified level. Therefore, I am terminating your services effective as of the end of the week. This has not been an easy decision for me. I have given it a lot of thought and feel it is best for both of us in the long run. I have reviewed my decision with both my manager and the personnel officer, and they both agree that it is a fair and proper decision."

Where you go next will depend upon the reaction you get. You may need only to listen to the person talk a while about what has happened. You may have to agree with the apparent injustice of it all. Following this reaction stage, move on as soon as you can to a positive outlook for the future and then summarize any appropriate administrative matters. These may include:

- Last day of work
- Handling final pay

109

- Handling employee benefits
- Reference checks
- Turning in company property

Conclude the discussion by offering to be of any help you can in the future and referring the individual to any other appropriate person for advice and counsel. For example, the personnel officer may be able to provide more details on benefit plan conversions or settlements and may be qualified to provide personal counseling.

Following the Discussion

As soon as the discussion is over, several items need immediate attention. First, write a detailed summary of what happened during the discussion. What did you tell the person? What were his or her reactions? Next, handle appropriate administrative work to remove the person properly from the payroll and initiate action to obtain a replacement. Finally, consider whether to tell the work group what has happened. Remember, news travels fast when someone leaves. Often the news is tainted with rumor, assumptions, and speculations. You might be better off to call your group together and state the facts briefly. This can underscore your willingness to deal with problems and your fairness. In turn this can remove some of the threat others may feel as a result of the experience.

CONCLUSION

No supervisor enjoys terminating the services of a group member. Many people put it off, hoping things will improve, and thereby avoid the unpleasant experience. There are many reasons for this, including an admission of your own poor judgment in selecting someone who did not work out. Everyone makes mistakes, but it takes special courage to admit them and take corrective action. When a termination decision is dragged out or ignored, it often becomes the subject of work-group gossip. On the other hand, when faced and handled with dignity and fairness, the experience can have a positive effect on the group. The work group will respect and admire you for accepting the full responsibility of your position. Your group would much rather see you as courageous and fair than cowardly and capricious. Negative reactions to a termination experience can have serious consequences. The affected individual may go to work for a competitor and divulge valuable information to the new employer. He or she may file a lawsuit. The company's reputation may be tarnished, causing serious effects on recruiting efforts and community image. Remaining group members may experience a decline in morale and loyalty. Therefore, it is certainly in the company's best interests to handle terminations as positively and sensitively as possible.

SUGGESTIONS
- Face your responsibilities of maintaining a work group of capable, willing members.
- Be willing to terminate the services of those who do not measure up.
- Be fair, equitable, and objective in making decisions to terminate someone's services.
- Handle the discussion with dignity, understanding, and a positive outlook.
- Do not neglect the employee and community relations impact of terminations.

Part IV
Working with Groups

- Staffing Your Work Group
- Organizing Your Work Group
- Using The Talent in Your Group
- Making Decisions That Get Results
- Conducting Work-Group Meetings
- Improving Productivity
- Handling Group Member Complaints
- Building an Effective Team

19

Staffing Your Work Group

CHAPTER HIGHLIGHTS
- The three steps in hiring new group members
- Three pitfalls to avoid when selecting among candidates
- Suggestions on picking group members for promotion

Selecting the right people to fill positions in your work group is one of the most important parts of your job as supervisor. Those persons you invite into your group as well as those you advance to more responsible positions make your job more or less difficult. For example, 80 to 90 percent of all nonperformance problems can be traced to poor selection and placement. People are not being matched properly to the jobs they are asked to perform.

SELECTING CANDIDATES FOR EMPLOYMENT

The selection process is straightforward, even though it may be difficult to carry out. It involves three key elements: determining job requirements, assessing candidate qualifications to fulfill those requirements, and choosing among available candidates.

Determining Job Requirements

The starting place for any selection and placement procedure is to determine what you are seeking. Look at the job to be filled and draw up a list of qualities required to fill it successfully. Focus attention on qualities that spell the difference between success and failure and list them in terms of action or behavior. Avoid generalities such as high school graduation. Instead, look at specifics such as operating appropriate machinery, working as part of a team, reading, writing, or calculating.

Assessing Candidate Qualifications

With an understanding of what you seek in a candidate, the next step is to determine the extent to which candidates fulfill

115

the requirements. This process is best viewed as a situation where you are trying to learn of any factors that would inhibit a candidate's chances of success. Understandably, the candidate often is determined to conceal those factors from you. There typically are three sources of data available to you during this step.

Background Investigation. The single most important indicator of how a person will perform in the future is how he or she has performed in the past. Individuals with a history of success tend to continue to be successful. Those with poor work records tend to be poor performers. Check and verify as much of the information as possible. Talk with schools and places of prior employment. When you do so, ask about work habits and quality of performance as well as the nature of the job assignment.

Interview. The purpose of the interview is to go beyond information normally written on the application. You want to learn specific skills, abilities, interests, motivations, and potential problems. To accomplish this, be very careful how you phrase your questions. Do not lead or direct the candidate's response. Following are examples of questions that should get you some worthwhile information. Use them as a model for forming other questions relevant to your job, work group, and location.

- Describe what you did in your last job.
- What did you enjoy most about it?
- What did you enjoy least?
- Of the bosses you have had, think of the one you most enjoyed working with. What did he or she do that you liked?
- Which boss did you least enjoy?
- How would you handle . . . (state a typical job task)?
- How will you get to work if you are hired?

Testing. Testing is the third source of information you can draw upon when assessing candidates' qualifications. The Equal Employment Opportunity Commission is concerned about fairness in testing, but that does not rule out this source of information. Rather, it requires tests to be job related and not to exclude a larger share of minority or women applicants. The best way to avoid problems with testing is to use job skills tests or simulations.

For example, if you are assessing typing candidates, have them type material similar to what they will face on the job. If you are assessing candidates for a supervisory position, give them a collection of typical problems to handle. See how they organize their effort, set priorities, and make decisions. Then evaluate the quality of the decisions they make.

Choosing Among Candidates

Choosing among candidates is the final step in the selection process. To increase the quality of these final decisions, consider all available, relevant information, match candidates' qualifications to the job requirements, and compare candidates to each other.

Comparing Candidates. To compare candidates, a system or format is necessary to keep your attention focused on relevant data. The following form will help you organize your information. Use it as a guide to develop one appropriate for the job you are filling. (The usefulness of such a form can be improved by weighting the importance of the job requirements. Then multiply factor ratings by weightings to arrive at a total evaluation.)

Pitfalls to Avoid. This sort of structure helps you avoid many of the potential pitfalls that might lead to incorrect conclusions. Here are the major ones to watch:

- *More is better.* There is a tendency to be impressed with overly qualified candidates. Hiring overly qualified candidates, however, often results in boredom, which leads to turnover or other personnel problems.
- *Irrelevancies.* Occasionally, you may be impressed with a candidate for reasons totally unrelated to the job you have to fill. For example, a secretarial candidate may take shorthand at 150 words a minute but this is irrelevant if your office uses dictating machines.
- *Biases.* Everyone has biases. When you are responsible for selecting candidates, learn your biases and work to minimize their effect on your decisions. Some to avoid particularly are related to physical appearance—height, weight, deformities, and attractiveness. There are also role biases such as against

117

CANDIDATE ASSESSMENT SUMMARY JOB: Office Assistant/Receptionist								
Instructions: Rate each factor from a low of 1 to high of 5. **CANDIDATE**	TYPING SKILLS	FILING SKILL	LANG. SKILL	CONGENIALITY	APPEARANCE	MATURITY	DEPENDABILITY	INTEREST	TOTAL
1.									
2.									
3.									
4.									
5.									
6.									
7.									
8.									
9.									
10.									

working mothers or divorced people. Some biases cause you to favor candidates, for example, those who served in the military, who worked their way through school, or who are from broken homes.

SELECTING CANDIDATES FOR PROMOTION

Many promotions are made for the wrong reasons, the most common being reward for past performance. This results in an excellent salesperson becoming a poor sales manager or an excellent craftsman becoming a poor foreman. The organization loses on both ends of the deal.

To overcome these problems, shift attention from past performance to the candidate's potential to fill the future assignment successfully. Follow the same set of procedures used in initial employment: define job requirements, assess candidates' qualifications to fulfill those requirements, then choose among available candidates. In the process of following these procedures, the same potential pitfalls exist and should be avoided.

Only two basic differences exist between an initial employment decision and a promotion decision. One is the limit on the potential field of candidates. Promotion candidates are limited to those already on the payroll and may be further limited to certain departments or fields of expertise. The other difference is that you have more information on the candidate as to qualifications and interests.

CONCLUSION

When the costs of recruiting are added to the costs of initial training, personnel turnover becomes a very significant expense to many organizations. Likewise, errors in promotion decisions are expensive in efficiency losses and personal losses as some group members face failure and demotion.

To minimize these costs, a rational selection procedure must be developed. Careful thought must be directed to identifying actual job requirements. Then candidates' qualifications must be assessed carefully and a decision must be made to select the best match between job requirements and qualifications.

Past practices of hiring and promoting people for the wrong reasons must be stopped if they in fact existed in your organization. Hire qualified candidates, but avoid placing overly qualified ones in jobs that lead to boredom and frustration. Only consider qualities relevant to the job, carefully avoiding personal biases. Likewise, when making promotions the most important part of the decision should be whether the candidate can perform the duties of the future job assignment.

SUGGESTIONS
- Draw up a list of job requirements for the starting positions in your group.
- Check out background data on candidates you are seriously considering.
- Consider using job-related skills tests as part of your selection process.
- Know and avoid your personal biases; stay with relevant qualifications.
- Base promotions on qualifications to perform the future job.

20

Organizing Your Work Group

CHAPTER HIGHLIGHTS
- Two suggested times to reorganize a work group
- Three approaches to reorganization
- Three things to examine when reorganizing
- Six principles of organization
- Three standard organizational models

Organization brings order to the work place. With order comes improved efficiency and better working relationships. Organizing assembles and arranges all of the resources of the group so the required work can be accomplished. Organization comes about because there is more work to be done than one person can handle. When many minds, hands, and skills are assembled, they must be coordinated to get the work done and to provide satisfaction for each member of the group. The results of organization should be greater than the sum of each of the individual parts.

Some supervisors have more freedom than others to reorganize their work group. Operate within the freedom you have either to change or to recommend changing your group's organization to improve its effectiveness. When considering reorganization, the following ideas will be helpful.

WHEN TO REORGANIZE

Change is often unsettling. People caught up in change frequently experience stress and, as a result, may resist your efforts. Therefore, reorganization should not occur too often. When it does happen, have a well-thought-out, complete plan rather than take a piecemeal approach. Logically, you should at least consider reorganizing at the following times.

Upon Initial Appointment

When you are initially appointed as supervisor of a new work group, consider how well it is organized. Frequently a new, different perspective will highlight opportunities for improvement. Your predecessor may have recognized a need for change but did not believe the timing to be right. Or your predecessor may have thought no improvement was necessary. In any event you have an excellent opportunity when you take over as the new supervisor to improve the organization of your group.

When Change Occurs

Work groups often experience changes that require an organizational change to maintain effectiveness. The three following changes are the most frequent ones experienced.

Growth. Success usually brings growth. In turn, growth dictates a need to evaluate and perhaps change organization. More people may require more levels of supervision, realignment of job duties, and reorganization of facilities. In addition to growth bringing more people into the work place, it may also dictate a dispersion of people either to added shift schedules or to different work sites. These changes will offer special opportunities when considering reorganization.

Diversification. When a work group takes on new duties, it should consider reorganizing in order to handle the new areas of responsibility effectively.

Technological Change. Changing technology typically heralds change in organization. New equipment usually has greater capacity than the old equipment it replaced. Therefore, fewer people may be needed to maintain the group's output. A look at organization at the same time new equipment is introduced may suggest several opportunities for improvement.

HOW TO REORGANIZE

Planning and carrying out your reorganization effort requires consideration of who should handle the project, what should be examined, and some elementary principles.

Who Should Be Involved?

You have several choices when deciding who should handle your reorganization project. The following three are the most common. (Regardless of who handles the project, you will of course need your management's support and approval.)

Do It Yourself. Depending on the scope and complexity of the project and your individual background, you might be quite capable of handling the project yourself.

Consultant. When you lack the time or expertise to handle the project on your own, consider engaging a consultant to work with you. The consultant could be either an internal or external person. Many larger companies have staff specialists available to assist in these projects. Consultants frequently bring experience and objectivity to a project that contribute to improved results. However, do not give up your authority. You are responsible for any changes made and have to live with the results long after the consultant has moved on.

Study Team. Another approach to organizational change that is finding wider acceptance today is to select a study team from your group to develop a proposal for your consideration and approval. This allows direct input to the project from those affected by it. This, in turn, develops a heightened sense of commitment to see that the change effort succeeds. The study team could be supplemented with either an internal or external consultant.

What to Examine

Four components of a work group must be examined when considering reorganization: the work, the group members, the relationships among group members and with interfacing groups, and the physical environment.

The Work. The activities or tasks of the group form the foundation of the organization. Because work is distributed among group members, it must be divided. Common ways to divide the work include considering the similarity of skills and knowledge required and the degree of skills and knowledge required. Also worth considering is the efficiency to be gained from combining work in close proximity to avoid or reduce travel time between tasks. Three basic patterns of operative-level production exist:

- *Serial.* Production moves step by step to its completion, each step handled by a different person.
- *Subunit Assembly.* Several production steps are handled by one person.
- *Unit Assembly.* All of the steps involved in creating a finished product are handled by one person.

Group Members. Each person is assigned a portion of the total work. Preferably, the assignment will give full recognition to the individual's skills, interests, and experience. The inter-action pattern between the work and the person assigned to it bring about the development of various types of behavior. Usually people adjust to the work requirements and interaction patterns become stable. Two types of behavior emerge:

- *Formal Behavior*—that which results from following job descriptions, standard procedures, prescribed lines of authority, and formalized channels of communications.
- *Informal Behavior*—that which results from the interaction among people in the formal structure. Informal behavior relies on relationships and creativity to get the job done in the face of cumbersome formal procedures or the lack of specific procedures.

Relationshps. A work group is a social entity. It provides the setting for the satisfaction of the social needs of its members. This social dimension is vital to the success of the group. What group members do for each other either contributes to or detracts from the achievement of the group's purpose. Through organization, provide the opportunity for relationships to develop. Group influence is important in winning acceptance of your change effort. People tend to dislike change that threatens to destroy either accustomed behavior patterns or established social relationships. However, when change is either initiated or supported by the group, resistance is minimized.

The other dimension of relationships looks at interfacing work groups and their members. Generally, two-way rather than one-way relationships are more satisfying. People enjoy and gain from discussions about issues influencing them as well as factors affecting their jobs. Therefore, consider establishing contacts between people doing work and those for whom it is being done.

Environment. Environment here refers to all of the physical facilities affecting or used by members of your group in the performance of their work. Most significant from an organization point of view are location and layout of work space and tools. Are these factors contributing to a smooth flow of work, or do they create delays and contribute to confusion?

Principles of Organization

As you examine the four components just detailed, consider these principles. They will guide you to worthwhile results.

Purpose of the Group. All effort should be directed toward achieving your group's reason for existing. Every group exists to produce and deliver a product or service to a customer, either within your company or on the outside. Organize in a way to achieve this purpose most effectively.

Size of Units. Most people do not like to work in isolation. This prevents the satisfaction of social needs. On the other hand, groups in excess of 12 are difficult to form into social units. Stay somewhere within this range to develop a sense of belonging.

Logical Grouping of Tasks. Most people like to identify with the accomplishment of an end result rather than do a single step in a process. Yet there should not be too wide a spread in skill levels involved or too much dispersion of duties.

Scope of Decision Making. Freedom to decide issues pertaining to the work lets people use their minds and experience a sense of satisfaction and self worth. Provide opportunity for planning, problem solving, and self-control.

Degree of Specialization. Jobs that are too specialized rob people of the opportunity to see how their effort relates to the whole and to experience a sense of accomplishment. However, underspecialization removes the opportunity for growth and the prestige of being an expert.

Reporting Level. Most people enjoy reporting to a top level of the organization. This affords status to the person and to the

125

work being done. Take this into account and see that reporting levels are appropriate.

Three Options Worth Considering

Considering these principles of organization, the following three standard designs have emerged as models.

Job Enlargement. Job enlargement consolidates tasks at the same level of complexity. It is commonly called horizontal job loading. Job enlargement provides variety of task involvement and an opportunity to identify more closely with a finished product. It results in combining steps in a serial production process so there are fewer work stations in the total system or in adopting either a subunit or unit assembly process.

Job Enrichment. Job enrichment moves some of the traditional management functions to lower levels in the organization. It is commonly called vertical job loading. Job enrichment provides opportunity for planning, decision making, problem solving, and controlling to be added to the work. As a result, group members experience a greater sense of ownership in their output. This generally leads to increased work quality and personal satisfaction.

Work Teams. Work teams operate as a unit, are self-contained, and include all of the skills necessary for performing the work assigned to them. They typically enjoy freedom to organize their own efforts to suit their interests. This form of organization capitalizes on the social dimension of work-centered relationships. Work teams may be an ongoing approach to daily operations, or they may be ad hoc task teams brought together temporarily to address a particular task.

CONCLUSION

According to some critics, most jobs in the U.S. are better suited to robots than mature adults. With the increased use of technology, work has become more simplified, standardized, and routine. However, technology has also contributed to greater affluence and education and has increased levels of aspiration. As a result of these benefits, more people want jobs that let them make greater use of their education and provide a sense of satisfaction. One solution to this problem is to reorganize the work place, providing group members with additional responsibility for planning, setting up, and checking their own work; for making decisions about methods and procedures; for establishing their own work pace; and for dealing directly with those who receive the results of their effort.

Take the opportunity to consider how your group is organized to achieve its purpose. Is it an effective, satisfying place to spend eight hours each working day?

SUGGESTIONS

- Study how the components of your work group fit together—the work, the group members, the relationships, and the environment.
- Consider using outside help in your reorganization project.
- Consider ways to gain group support for your planned change.
- Do not reorganize too often; it is unsettling and may develop resistance.

21

Using the Talent in Your Group

CHAPTER HIGHLIGHTS
- Three levels of delegation
- General guidelines for successful delegation
- Four types of controls to monitor work in progress
- Suggestions on the benefits of delegation

Most work groups have talents, skills, and abilities that are never used because of restricted views of who should do what type of work. Involvement in decision making through delegation is an effective way to use these untapped resources.

To delegate or not to delegate is never the question. To get things done, you must learn to make effective use of this tool. It is the only way to broaden your span of influence beyond your ability to do the work personally. Delegation may well be the most difficult aspect of the art of good management. Yet the ability to delegate is one of the most important tools you have to ensure that your work is done efficiently and effectively.

LEVELS OF DELEGATION

Many supervisors who otherwise endorse delegation in principle do not delegate because they mistakenly see it as an all-or-nothing arrangement. However, this is not the case. The levels of delegation range from work pace to decision making. You decide which level is appropriate by considering the task, the ability of the person, the amount of top management interest, and the time available.

Level 1 Delegation. This is the beginning point on the way to full delegation. This level is appropriate for those who are unfamiliar with the full scope of job responsibilities. The actual delegation is limited to the rate, or pace, of work and decisions on acceptable levels of quality—that is, whether work measures up to minimum standards. At this level you tell someone what is to be done and how to do it.

Level 2 Delegation. Moving to this level provides greater freedom and opportunity for group members. This level of delegation is appropriate for those with demonstrated capability. Delegation at this level allows the individual to decide how things are to be done, at what pace to meet agreed upon deadlines, and whether or not work meets quality standards. Within this level a group member has the opportunity to study a situation, develop a plan to resolve a problem, and sell you on the plan's merits.

Level 3 Delegation. At this level the group member is given an area of responsibility and the freedom to make decisions within it. There is still opportunity to discuss and direct or confirm the goals or objectives to be achieved. But beyond that, the individual decides what to do and how to do it.

Under most circumstances, full delegation should be your goal. It means the group member has been given an area of decision making and the decisions are accepted. To reach this level, you must be willing to relinquish part of your authority. You must be willing to gamble that your group members can do a better job when left on their own than when closely supervised. If you play safe and avoid risk by not delegating, you merely make your group an extension of yourself rather than the separate, competent people they are capable of becoming.

HOW TO DELEGATE

Delegation is both personal and individual. As such, it depends to a large extent on the relationship between you and your group members as well as their ability and interest.

General Guidelines

Some general guidelines apply to all situations:
- Be clear in the level of delegation you are granting.
- Set standards to measure results against expectations.
- Give the group member all of the relevant information you have about the task.

129

- Delegate only to qualified members of your group. This may mean that you will have to train some of them in preparation for further delegation.
- Establish controls that will alert you to exceptions to normal operations.

Establish Controls

Full delegation does not mean that you cut a person loose and say, "Okay, you're on your own. Go to it." You must provide standards and controls. Controls provide the opportunity to examine actual performance against standards and to take whatever action is necessary. The following possibilities should give you some ideas for your operations.

Personal Inspection. When a tangible product or service is the output of your group, you can assess the group's effectiveness through periodic personal inspections. Such visits, however, should be unannounced to be most effective.

Visual Display. Graphs and charts can be maintained to compare actual to expected results. This works particularly well for sales, production, and expense control.

Status Reports. Group members can be asked to provide private, periodic reports of results either orally or in writing.

Work-Group Meetings. Your group can meet and discuss the results of the department against standards or objectives. This is particularly appropriate when people must work together to achieve common results.

Getting Started

The first thing to do if you are interested in delegating is to analyze your involvement in the work of your group. In this analysis, place all of the work you now perform into three categories:

- Work that can only be done by you.
- Work that can be delegated immediately.
- Work that can be delegated as soon as someone is ready to do it.

Then evaluate each group member's readiness for delegation. Two things must be considered: ability to do the work and interest in doing it well. Has the person done this type of work before?

If so, what was the outcome? Were quality, quantity, cost, and timeliness up to standard?

Work you are now performing that can be delegated immediately should be assigned to group members at the appropriate degree of delegation. As you acquire confidence in their abilities, increase the delegation until you have accomplished as near-complete delegation as possible.

When you have identified work that can be delegated but no one is ready to perform, you have identified training and development needs in your group. Set out immediately to prepare someone to perform these duties. Then proceed to delegate by levels until full delegation has been achieved. If it is a lack of ability, provide training in the skills involved. If it is a lack of interest, provide work assignments with clear performance expectations. Then follow up and provide feedback on performance.

BENEFITS OF DELEGATION

One of the most marked effects of delegation is the feeling of self-respect it gives group members. When you give people a task to perform and let them decide how it should be done, you make it plain that they're capable and they gain importance and self-confidence. There is no greater motivating force than to put someone in charge of a portion of a department's work, delegate the authority required to make decisions that spell success or failure, then provide rewards in line with accomplishments.

As supervisor, you also receive benefits from delegating. The most obvious is the time that is freed for managing—more time planning the future of your group, coordinating the efforts of your staff, developing new and better techniques to do the work, and establishing better relationships with those you deal with in your day-to-day contacts.

CONCLUSION

Effective delegation may well be the most difficult task for new supervisors. However, your success depends on your mastering the skills required.

The best place to begin is to analyze your involvement in the day to day work of your group and identify that which can be delegated. Then, assess the skills and interests of your group members. Now you are ready to begin a methodical process of training and delegation until each group member has been given authority over a portion of the group's work. Don't forget to include controls and monitoring techniques in the process.

SUGGESTIONS

- Analyze the work you do to see what can be delegated.
- Delegate as much as possible using the appropriate level of delegation.
- Strive to reach full delegation with your most capable staff members.

22

Making Decisions That Get Results

CHAPTER HIGHLIGHTS
- A six step rational decision process
- Four reasons for involving others in decision making
- Five levels of involvement for others in decision making

Making decisions is a part of everyday life. Some are made by default, i.e., a decision is delayed to the point that some other event removes the opportunity for decision. Others are made on the basis of feelings or emotions and are often made in haste. Finally, some decisions are carefully thought out and made on the basis of facts and logic.

Which of these approaches results in the best decisions? You have probably made good decisions using each of them. However, the odds are better for your making a good decision when facts and logic form its foundation.

A good decision gets good results. Good results can be expected when a decision meets three requirements: it is of high quality, has the support of those who will fulfill it, and is reached within a reasonable time. To make decisions that consistently meet these requirements, you must address two issues: a procedure to follow in making decisions and the extent to which others should be involved in the process.

A RATIONAL DECISION PROCEDURE

To avoid jumping to conclusions, a rational procedure should be followed when making decisions. This procedure is designed to move you away from feelings-based decisions toward decisions based on facts and logic.

Study the Situation. The starting point is to study the situation to be sure you are deciding the proper issue. Time invested

133

in this step will pay off handsomely later. At this point make sure you have identified the real problem and that you have all of the available facts.

State an Objective. Now state what you want to accomplish. Your objective should be in terms of end results, and it should avoid any reference to how you plan to get there.

Establish Imperatives. Imperatives are the absolute essentials that must be built into the final decision for it to be acceptable, e.g., a restriction against increasing the size of the work group. The fewer imperatives the better because they restrict the range of alternatives. On the other hand, if they exist, it is best to get them out in the open early.

Generate Alternatives. Now it is time to make a list of all of the possible ways to reach your objective. Do not screen out any possibilities; leave that until later. Jot down even the craziest ideas because they often will remind you of other, more reasonable alternatives.

Determine Evaluation Criteria. After you have thought of all of the ideas you can, you need a way to sort through and evaluate them. In this step you determine how that will be done. Select three or four criteria against which each alternative will be measured, e.g., feasibility, cost, availability, or contribution to objective.

Evaluate Alternatives. Take each of the alternatives and evaluate it against each criterion. Where data are available, fill in the data—for example, cost and availability figures. Where data are not available, make a subjective assessment such as high, moderate, or low. This would apply to criteria such as feasibility and contribution to objectives.

Decide. The final step in the rational decision procedure is to study your evaluation of alternatives and select the best course of action available to you. Obviously, there is no requirement that you choose the alternative that looks best in the evaluation. Consider the consequences of different alternatives and the probability of undesirable consequences occurring. If you choose other than the best evaluated alternative, understand your reasons for doing so.

INVOLVING OTHERS IN THE DECISION

When faced with a decision opportunity, you have three choices of how to handle it: you can make the decision by yourself, you can involve others with you, or you can delegate the decision to someone else. To make the best choice, consider the reasons for involving others and the extent to which they should be involved.

Reasons for Involving Others

There are four good reasons for involving others in the decision. If none of these reasons exist, make the decision on your own.

Information. Probably the most important reason for involving others is that you do not have all of the information you need to reach a good decision. When this is the case, obtain and use the information you need.

Commitment. The next most important reason for involving others is to gain their commitment to carry out the decision. This suggests two considerations. First, is the commitment of others required? Occasionally you will be the one to carry out the decision, making the commitment of others unnecessary. Second, can you count on the commitment of others without their involvement? If you have a track record of making good decisions in the area you are presently concerned with, you probably can count on the support and commitment you need without involving others in the decision.

Creativity. Some situations lend themselves to many possible decision alternatives. In these cases, groups usually can create more possibilities than individuals can. When you face a decision where there does not appear to be any reasonable answer, assemble a group and explore the possibilities.

Development. Occasionally you will find an opportunity to involve others simply for their own education and development. You have the knowledge and experience to handle the matter, but in the future they will have to handle similar cases on their own. Get them involved and guide them through a proper analysis and decision.

Extent of Involvement

Several degrees of involvement exist. Each can be appropriate under the right set of circumstances. The following ideas will help you choose the best one for your situation.

135

Decide Alone. The least involvement is obviously none. Here you make the decision alone. This choice is proper when none of the reasons listed above exist. It may also be used properly when time does not permit involving others. When this happens, it is best to talk with the others later and explain why you found it necessary to act on your own.

Discuss Individually. This is the least amount of actual involvement. It is appropriate when you need information on which to base a good decision. It also is a good choice when circumstances prevent meeting as a group, e.g., if people cannot leave other duties at the same time or they are spread over a large geographic area. These discussions can be in person or by phone.

Discuss in a Meeting. This degree of involvement lets you take full advantage of the information and ideas of others. It is particularly appropriate when you need some creative ideas but feel you must make the final decision.

Join in the Decision. This degree of involvement usually results in the highest feeling of commitment by those involved. Therefore, it is appropriate when a high degree of commitment is required. It also takes full advantage of information held by group members and the creative potential of the group. When this choice is selected, follow the rational decision procedure as the agenda for your meeting.

Turn Over to Others. Occasionally, the best choice will be to turn the situation over to others to decide. It can be given to an individual or to a group. For this to be a successful choice, they must be interested in and willing to make the decision, and you must be willing to accept anything they decide. This means you must specify any imperatives you have in advance of their making the decision.

CONCLUSION

You can make good decisions that have the commitment of those who must fulfill them. To do so, be sure you have identified the proper issue for decision; then handle it in a logical rather than an emotional way.

The quality of a decision depends on the information used in making it. See that you have enough accurate information to make a sound choice.

Commitment to support and fulfill a decision depends on the extent of involvement by those whose commitment is needed. Provide opportunity to those whose commitment you need to have a voice in the decision process. This requires more than just casual opportunity for comment; it requires a chance to make a difference in the final decision.

Time needs to be viewed in its total perspective. It may not take you long to make a decision, but you may spend considerable time selling others on its merits for it to be carried out properly. However, decision-making meetings may go on and on but may have commitment as an outcome of the meeting. When involvement is appropriate to gain support and commitment, minimize the total time investment by exercising leadership over the decision-making meeting. (See Chapter 23.)

High-quality decisions that enjoy the necessary commitment to implement them made with a minimum time investment should be your goal. This goal can be reached by following a rational decision procedure and appropriately involving others in the process.

SUGGESTIONS

- Do not put off making decisions that must be made.
- Think through problems before attempting to make a decision.
- Consider several alternatives before making a final decision.
- Involve others in the decision process when appropriate.

23
Conducting Work-Group Meetings

CHAPTER HIGHLIGHTS
- Four types of meetings with suggestions for success
- Considerations in preparing for a meeting
- Four keys to conducting successful meetings
- Three responsibilities following meetings

Most people cringe at the thought of sitting through another meeting because most waste time, often do not accomplish anything worthwhile, and therefore are frustrating. Your meetings need not fall into this pattern. With a little advance planning and some attention to what takes place, you can run meetings that get things done. The following ideas will help you achieve this goal.

BEFORE THE MEETING
Before your meeting ever gets underway, the foundation is laid for its success or failure. To ensure success, see that these issues are handled properly.

Be Sure a Meeting is Necessary
Many meetings should never be called. Consider your objective. What are you trying to accomplish? Then consider if a meeting is the best way to achieve that objective. There are alternatives to holding a meeting. For example, would it be better to make a few phone calls, write a memorandum, or meet individually with the people involved?

Pick the Best Time
Some meetings fail because they are too far removed from the event they are concerned with or are called for the wrong day of the week or time during the day. To hold participant interest, the subject of your meeting should be very high on their priority list. If it must compete for attention, it may lose. Consider other

demands on the participants such as work deadlines, operating problems, and personal issues.

Determine the Kind of Meeting Needed

Meetings come in four basic types. Each type is designed to accomplish a different purpose and is run quite differently.

Information Meetings. Information meetings pass on information to those in attendance. They may be attended by a large number of people who listen to what is said. Little opportunity exists for questions. The one running these meetings must be well prepared in order to hold interest and communicate clearly.

Discussion Meetings. Discussion meetings are used to share ideas, opinions, feelings, and information about a particular topic in order to ensure complete understanding. They do not result in a decision or action plan. Discussion meetings have two typical applications. One is where the person calling the meeting wants to clarify something with those in attendance, for example, a procedure or policy. The other application is where the one calling the meeting wants to understand the viewpoints of those attending before making a decision. To be successful, the meeting size should be limited to 12 participants, and a positive, supportive climate should exist so people feel comfortable voicing their ideas.

Problem-solving Meetings. Problem-solving meetings pool the information and knowledge of those in attendance. When you are unsure of the cause of a problem or there are several ways to handle it, a meeting can result in the best solution. These meetings should be limited to seven people who can contribute worthwhile information. A positive climate is necessary, and a structured, orderly process is required to identify the problem and generate solution alternatives.

Decision-making Meetings. When a decision will need the support of others to be carried out successfully, a decision-making meeting should be held. Decision-making meetings vary in size, based on the number of people whose support is needed. When the group is larger than ten, voting is probably the best way to reach a decision. (The group may set a higher than simple majority vote requirement, for example, two-thirds or three-quarters.)

139

With ten members or less, discussion and agreement is usually a satisfactory procedure.

Select Attendees

As a general rule of thumb, you want the smallest number of appropriate people in attendance. Consider the objective of your meeting. If you want to solve a problem, you need people who can contribute knowledge. If you want to make a decision, you need people with authority who have a stake in the outcome. If you are relating information, who needs to know? If you are holding a discussion, who is affected and who can contribute? Having decided upon the appropriate people to attend, give them a specific, clear invitation to the meeting.

Prepare an Agenda

All meetings need an agenda. Attendees need to know what will be dealt with and approximately how much time to set aside for the meeting. If possible, check ahead of time with participants for their ideas of what should be included on the agenda.

Arrange the Meeting Place

The meeting room and any equipment should be planned and reserved well in advance of your meeting. Participants need comfortable seating, adequate space, and proper lighting and ventilation.

The room arrangement should support the type of meeting you plan to conduct. As a guideline, you want those who will be talking to each other to be able to maintain eye contact. Therefore, auditorium or classroom-style seating is okay for information or discussion meetings. However, in problem-solving and decision-making meetings, a circular arrangement is preferred.

DURING THE MEETING

Your attitude and activities during the meeting set its tone and contribute to or detract from its quality. You want to accomplish your objective in the least amount of time without anyone feeling railroaded or ignored. You want participants to leave the meeting feeling that something worthwhile was achieved. To do this, several issues need your attention.

140

Manage the Time Dimension

As a standard, use the first 15 minutes of your meeting as effectively as the last 15 minutes. Start promptly, address the purpose of the meeting, and adjourn when you have achieved your purpose.

Occasionally you may have more information to cover than you feel there is time available. In this case, involve the group in prioritizing the items on your agenda. Then address the items in order. If time runs out, you will have handled the most important ones.

Clearly State the Meeting's Purpose

Even though you have an agenda, all participants may not agree on the meeting's purpose. To overcome this problem, start with a statement of purpose. Any misunderstandings can then be resolved rather than having them interfere later with the meeting's progress.

Exercise Leadership

There is a middle ground between directing or ramrodding a meeting and letting it drift out of control. That middle ground is leadership. Good meetings have leadership; bad meetings do not. Some of the necessary activities of a leader include the following, depending on the type of meeting you are having.

Keep on the Topic. One of the most common complaints about meetings is that they drift off the topic. Keep attention focused on an issue until it is resolved or until the group agrees to set it aside. Use your agenda to screen out unrelated conversations.

Manage Air Time. Some participants may want to do all of the talking while others seem to have nothing to say. Make room in the discussion and involve those who are less participative.

Elicit Information. People tend to express conclusions without sharing background information that led to their opinion. Ask probing questions to learn why they feel as they do or want to do as they propose.

Compare Points of View. When several ideas are proposed to solve a problem or reach a decision, compare the ideas—show where they are alike and different. Then encourage the development of other alternatives that reduce the differences.

141

Integrate and Test for Decision. After considerable discussion, a meeting often drifts because no one states a conclusion. As leader, accept this task. Integrate the various ideas and suggestions you have heard and propose a decision on the issue. It may not be the final decision, but it gets people working toward one.

Watch for Loss of Attention. Pay attention to your group for nonverbal signals that suggest members are losing attention. When you notice this, make some changes in the way the meeting is going. For example, you can speak more loudly and more rapidly, ask questions, call a break, or adjourn.

Model Supportive Behavior. Do not embarrass or belittle anyone for participating in the meeting. Statements like, "That's a dumb idea," will stop discussion. Even when you feel a suggestion is short on quality, thank the person for speaking up.

Manage Conflict. Occasionally two or more people may differ strongly on how something should be done. An effective leader will help them work through this by being sure they understand each other, by identifying the imperatives in their proposals, and by using other group members to formulate additional alternatives. Occasionally discussion may become so heated that it will be best to leave the subject for awhile. When this seems to be the situation, table the issue until later in the meeting or call for a brief break.

Summarize Accomplishments

End every meeting with a summary of what was accomplished during the meeting. Participants often fail to recognize what benefit exists from having been part of the meeting; your summary should make it clear. As appropriate, include a review of decisions made and actions planned and who has agreed to do what by when.

AFTER THE MEETING

Your responsibilities do not end with adjournment. Three general areas of responsibility still remain.

Evaluate the Meeting

Evaluation is an important part of the growth and development process. All meetings should be examined from the perspective of how they could be run better next time. There are three general ways to accomplish an evaluation.

Questionnaire. You can distribute a questionnaire or evaluation form to all of the participants. Study the responses to identify improvement opportunities. Alternatively, you could summarize the questionnaire responses and at your next meeting spend some time discussing ways to improve.

Interview. You may choose to visit with participants in person or by telephone to get their critique of your meeting. Again, summarize the responses and look for improvement opportunities.

Self-Critique. The minimum evaluation effort would be to review the experience personally and privately. This could lead you to observations of where improvement might be needed. You certainly will know if the meeting room was adequate or if the time allocation was appropriate. You may not know, however, how people react to your leadership or if some important topic was left off the agenda.

Distribute Action Plan Summary

Compile and distribute a list of decisions made and action plans resolved. It is unnecessary to provide complete minutes of most meetings in business and industry. However, a memorandum of discussion is an important part of any meeting where agreements were made. It prevents different views of what was decided from emerging as time passes and memories wane.

Take Agreed-upon Action

If you agreed to do anything during the meeting, carry it out. Avoiding things leads to neglect. It also suggests to the other person a lack of interest.

CONCLUSION

Business meetings need not be a waste of time. All that is required is for you to manage this part of your responsibilities the same as you manage other parts—by planning, organizing, leading, and controlling. For successful meetings, be sure a meeting is required; then plan for it, develop an agenda, exercise leadership during the meeting, and follow up after the meeting to see that all agreements are carried out.

SUGGESTIONS
- Have an agenda for all meetings.
- Limit attendance to the minimum necessary people.
- Exercise leadership during the meeting.
- Manage time during the meeting.
- Compile and distribute a list of decisions and action plans.

24
Improving Productivity

CHAPTER HIGHLIGHTS
- A model for analyzing group productivity
- Suggestions for examining your group's output
- Four suggestions for improving your group's operation
- Suggestions for examining what your group uses in producing its output

A great deal of concern has been voiced about the decline in productivity in America. This concern is so widespread that all supervisors are responsible to take a close look at their operations. Where can gains be made in the effectiveness and efficiency of operations under your supervision?

As a starting point, consider the following drawing:

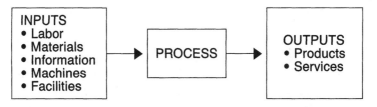

INPUTS
- Labor
- Materials
- Information
- Machines
- Facilities

PROCESS

OUTPUTS
- Products
- Services

Every work group takes something in the form of input, does something to it, and produces a product or service that is delivered to someone else. Productivity considers each of these three areas and measures the results in terms of the ratio of output to input. Productivity gains are experienced when the same level of input results in more output; reduced levels of input result in the same output; an increase in input results in a larger increase in output; and a decrease in input results in a smaller decrease in output.

When looking for opportunities for gains in productivity, analyze each of the three areas. It generally is easier to work backward through the system—first looking at output, then process, and finally input.

OUTPUT—WHAT YOU PRODUCE

A consideration of what you produce leads to an analysis of your group's effectiveness. Are you turning out products or services that make a contribution to your customer, either outside buyers or inside users of your output?

If your customers are outside your own company, competition in the marketplace helps monitor your effectiveness. If you can sell your product at a profit, you are effective. However, you should consider whether you could turn a better profit by modifying your output, modifying the package, or delivering it differently.

If your customers are inside your company, three questions are worth exploring. Is all of the output you deliver essential to the operation of the business? Any group that has been in existence for several years is probably producing something that is unnecessary. It may be nice to know or have, but it is really not needed. If you provide reports, for example, are they used or are they simply received and filed? Next, consider the form in which your output is provided to others. Can it be redesigned to be utilized better by your customer? Finally, consider whether you should exist as a group. When you have identified your essential output and its most effective form, decide whether someone else, either inside or outside your company, could deliver the product or service at less cost. You may find that you must become more effective or turn your part of the business over to someone else.

PROCESS—WHAT YOU DO

An analysis of what you do as a work group and how you do it directs your attention to the efficiency of your operation. Four areas deserve particular attention.

Job Design

Consider the tasks or activities you have grouped into each job. (See Chapter 20.) Is there opportunity for employees to do interesting and varied tasks to avoid boredom? Often the most efficient way to divide work in the short run loses in the long run due to boredom. Do individuals turn out an identifiable product or are they only doing one minor step in the production process? Job enrichment has contributed substantially to productivity through more interesting work. Key elements in the process are:

- Forming natural work units.
- Combining tasks into complete jobs.
- Establishing client relationships when appropriate.
- Moving decision making down to the lowest possible level.
- Opening feedback channels.

Some very positive productivity gains have been experienced by assigning production teams to complete a product then allowing team members to decide who should do the various tasks. Does your work lend itself to this arrangement?

Goals with Feedback

Another way to increase productivity is to set production output goals and let people know how they are doing relative to them. To be effective, goals need to be realistic, and it helps if group members have a voice in setting them. Without support from the group, the exercise is doomed to failure. Group goals stimulate cooperation within work groups and competition between groups. Individual goals promote competition among work-group members.

Procedures

Are members of your group using the most efficient ways to do things? Can procedures be simplified? This area encourages people to work smarter rather than harder. Again, get group members involved in looking at how they do things and seeking more efficient ways. Eliminate unnecessary activities and look for the easiest way to do what remains.

Planning and Scheduling

In some work groups many potentially productive hours are wasted waiting for materials or the services of others that are required to proceed with the work. Recognizing this, some offices schedule mail-handling personnel an hour earlier. When others

147

arrive, their morning mail is already on their desks. How can you improve your planning and scheduling to reduce or eliminate this kind of waste?

Inventories of materials and supplies are another area worth considering. Are items available when needed? Are purchases made in the most economical quantities, balancing quantity discounts against storage space and potential loss due to deterioration and obsolescence?

INPUT—WHAT YOU USE

What you use in producing the product or service you deliver offers many opportunities for improvement in productivity. While certainly not all-inclusive, the following ideas should help you think along the right lines.

Labor

The most important input in your production process is the talent and energy of the members of your work group. Do you have the proper number of people in the right mix of talent? For example, you might be able to increase your group's output substantially by adding a person. Is there a bottleneck somewhere? Do people have to wait for a particular service or activity? Another typist might increase the output of an office. A new mechanic might increase the output of a machine shop. Talk with those involved in the major activity of your group to see if support personnel are needed.

Next, consider the qualifications of people being hired into your group. Are applicants interested in the work and able to handle it? The average education in the work force today is fairly high. This frequently leads to hiring overly qualified candidates who soon become bored or leave for other jobs. In either case, the effectiveness and efficiency of your group is affected.

Finally, look at the training provided to prepare new group members to assume their jobs. (See Chapter 12 on training.) Ideally, you can hire people with the knowledge and experience to become immediate contributing members of your group.

However, you seldom will enjoy this ideal. Usually some training will be required. See that it is well designed and presented to teach the skills required for effective performance.

Materials

An analysis of your material's input should examine both the form and source. Are there materials available that would be easier to work with and more reliable or that would require fewer steps to convert to output? Are more reliable, economical sources available? Can contracts be negotiated to reduce unit costs? Would your supplier be willing to customize your materials or their packaging to make handling easier? Can more economical delivery methods be used?

Information

As with materials, an analysis of your information input should consider both its form and source. Is the information you need available when you need it? Are you getting what you need or are you getting too much so that time is wasted sorting through and/or consolidating information? Are the most efficient means being used to transmit information? Computers and FAX machines are a lot faster than mail delivery. Consider all of the available possibilities.

Machines

Computer technology has expanded the capabilities of machines. Two significant areas of application are storage and retrieval of information and computerized control of other machines. What opportunities exist for you to increase your group's effectiveness by replacing existing machines with more reliable, more efficient ones? Where can human effort be replaced with machines in routine, repetitive tasks? Frequently, computer-based information systems are faster and more reliable.

When considering the range of opportunities in this area, do not go overboard. Idle machine capacity ordinarily is not a wise investment. If a typist can do the work you need on a standard electric typewriter, there is no need to invest in a computer-based word processing system. However, if the computer-based system could do the work of several typists, it could be a wise move.

Facilities

Facilities need to be adequate but not elaborate. Inadequate facilities are inefficient and lead to employee dissatisfaction. However, elaborate facilities do not contribute anything to productivity. In looking at facilities, three areas should be considered. First, is there enough space for the activities normally carried out by your group? Then consider the impact of the facilities on group members. Is there adequate temperature control, ventilation, and lighting? Are the facilities maintained and clean? Finally, consider the layout of work areas, restrooms, and central storage facilities to minimize confusion and wasted motion.

Taking the cost into account, would it be feasible to have off-site facilities such as warehouse space and meeting rooms? Based on frequency of use, would it be better to rent such space as needed rather than have it available but used infrequently?

CONCLUSION

Opportunities exist for improving productivity in most work groups. The way to go about it is to examine the total range of opportunities using the input-process-output model as a guide.

Many companies have experienced considerable success in this area by having people examine their own work practices. Sometimes this includes total work groups; other times it involves only representatives from the work group. In either case the purpose for doing so is to use their information and ideas in developing improvement plans and to gain their commitment to fulfill the plans developed.

When increasing productivity in any organization, it is important to consider the practices of the management/supervisory group. That group is a model and an example to everyone. If it is inefficient and overly self-indulgent, others will not be convinced of the need to be efficient and economical.

SUGGESTIONS
- Look for ways to improve the productivity of your work group.
- Involve group members in the search for increased effectiveness and efficiency.
- Model efficient, economical practices to your group.

25

Handling Group Member Complaints

CHAPTER HIGHLIGHTS
- Six suggestions to follow when taking complaints
- Seven steps to follow when answering complaints

Being attentive and responsive to complaints from members of your group is one of the best ways to maintain morale.

People often feel they have no way to influence events or circumstances that directly affect them. This leads to feelings of powerlessness. To help overcome these feelings, listen to the complaints they have, investigate them, and lend your support in resolving them. Even when an issue is not resolved to the individual's satisfaction, your willingness to listen and your help in looking into the matter will be appreciated.

TAKING COMPLAINTS

Your initial contact sets the stage for personal reactions to the experience. During this discussion you want to provide a comfortable, supportive feeling that says it is okay to talk about the issue of concern. You have two objectives during this discussion: get as much information as you can and allow the individual to voice any bad feelings surrounding the situation. Be careful not to take sides during this discussion. Remember, every story has at least two sides, and you are hearing only one of them.

Take All Complaints Seriously. No matter how minor or insignificant an issue seems to you, it is important to the person complaining about it. Do not brush anyone off lightly. Take enough time considering your response to demonstrate that you are taking the matter seriously.

Talk to People Right Away. When someone comes to see you with a complaint, make time to listen. If you are particularly busy at the moment, make an appointment to meet within a day or two. If you are indefinite or seem to put people off, they will think you are not interested.

Probe for Information. As a person describes a complaint, ask for whatever information you need to understand the issue and act upon it. Do not assume even the most obvious. Occasionally, people attempt to minimize their part in a problem by selectively omitting certain details. Probe beneath the surface to understand what is involved.

Listen for the Real Problem. The initial problem presented may not be the only or the most significant one. Sometimes the person may be checking your receptivity by mentioning a less-important issue. If you seem receptive, other issues will be introduced. Always ask, "Is there anything else you would like to talk about?" Other times, group members may be more concerned with how something was done than with what was done. Feelings have been hurt, but one cannot complain about hurt feelings. Being aware of this; listen for the real problem.

Do Not Make People Defend Their Complaints. Sure you need enough information to handle the complaint properly. But do not try to maneuver someone into admitting the complaint is unfounded. You must make it clear that you are interested in the problem and are concerned with fair treatment. Remember, the opportunity to complain is often more important than any resolution of the issue.

Tell the Person When to Expect Your Answer. If you cannot solve the problem immediately, discuss what you plan to do and when you will have an answer. Frequently, further investigation will be needed. For example, you may need to talk with someone in the personnel office regarding benefit plans or salary practices. You may have to talk to your boss to clarify some rule or procedure. Or you may have to talk to another group member involved in the situation. After your investigation, get back together as agreed. If, for any reason, you do not have an answer at that time, meet anyway. Explain why you do not have an answer and set a new date.

ANSWERING COMPLAINTS

How the group member feels at the end of this discussion will have a dramatic effect on work-group morale. Questions like "Are you really interested in my problems?" "Will you really go to bat for me?" "Are you really interested in fair treatment?" will probably be discussed within the work group shortly after your follow-up discussion. You want the person to leave your office with positive feelings about how you handled the matter.

Review What You Did. A good starting point often is to review what you did during the investigative stage. This will demonstrate the extent of your interest and your willingness to get involved.

Concentrate on What Is Right. People typically are irritated by party-line answers to their problems. Do not be concerned about who is right. This is not a matter of supporting management in wrong decisions but is a matter of dealing objectively with the facts in the case.

If You Were Wrong, Admit It. Everyone admires a person who can admit mistakes. Do not let personal pride lead you into fighting to maintain a bad decision.

Apologize if Appropriate. If, under the stress of the moment, you were rude or inconsiderate, do not be afraid to apologize. A sincere apology, when warranted, will go a long way in gaining you the respect of your work group.

If You Were Right, Explain Why. Often times complaints arise because of misunderstood rules, policies, or procedures. Take the opportunity to explain what happened and why it was appropriate. Also consider whether it would be worthwhile to advise everyone in your group about the rule, policy, or procedure involved. Maybe others do not understand it either.

Discuss the Matter Objectively. During the discussion stay with the facts about what you did and what the outcome was. Avoid language that might lead to negative attitudes. Do not belittle nor demean the other person.

Pave the Way for Discussions with Others. Sometimes it will be appropriate for a member of your group to talk to someone else about a complaint. When this is the case, make

154

the necessary arrangements for the discussion to take place. Find out specifically who should be seen, call that person, and set up an appointment. It is much more comfortable to discuss something when the way has been paved ahead of time. Do not hesitate to let someone talk to your boss, especially if the issue involved questions your authority or judgment.

CONCLUSION

Handling group member complaints must be fair and equitable, and it must be seen by others as fair and equitable. To accomplish this, two areas of concern need special attention. First, they must know about your interest and willingness to get involved. Take every opportunity to tell them—work-group meetings, private conversations, bulletin board notices. Second, they must feel they get a fair deal when they come to you with a problem. Your success depends upon your attitude in the discussion. Concentrate on being sincere, open, direct, and honest with people.

With this approach to handling complaints, you can have a positive impact on morale in your group. However, do not expect miracles overnight. You have to expect a slow start. People naturally will be suspicious of your motives at first. But with some positive experiences you will win the support of your group.

SUGGESTIONS
- Take every complaint seriously.
- Probe for details and listen for the real problem.
- Remain objective while handling a complaint.
- Investigate fully or refer the person to others as appropriate.
- Respond promptly.

26

Building An Effective Team

The key to your success as a supervisor is the relationship between you and your work group. You are dependent upon your group; you need it just as much as it needs you. Standing alone as one person in an organization, you will have little impact on the world in which you exist. However, when several people work together, great things can be achieved. Your task is to build a work group of willing, cooperative members who work together in a climate of acceptance, support, and trust.

CHARACTERISTICS OF AN EFFECTIVE TEAM

Effective teams experience high productivity and morale. They tend to develop into their own social systems and experience a high level of group loyalty. Occasionally they develop elitist attitudes, seeing themselves as better than other groups. They tend to display the following qualities:
  ● Favorable attitudes toward the organization, the management, and the work to be done.
  ● Highly motivated to do a good job.
  ● A tightly knit social system.
  ● Self-control and guidance.

Impact on Group Members

Group acceptance is important to most people, and they frequently are willing to conform to group behavior as the price they pay for acceptance. In this regard the work group serves a central role in the organization. The greater the attraction and loyalty to the group, the more individual members are motivated to do the following:

- Accept goals and decisions of the group.
- Seek to influence those goals and decisions by participating actively.
- Communicate openly and fully to group members.
- Welcome communication and influence from other members of the group.
- Help to achieve group goals.
- Seek support and recognition from other members of the group.

View of Supervision

Members of highly effective work groups generally have a positive view of supervision. The supervisor is seen as an important part of the total system. These groups tend to see their supervisors as:

- Supportive, friendly, and helpful.
- Having confidence in their ability and integrity.
- Having high performance expectations.
- Providing necessary training and coaching.
- Viewing errors as learning opportunities rather than chances to criticize.

THE ROLE OF SUPERVISOR

Your role in building an effective team begins with selecting and training qualified work-group members. Then allow them the opportunity to influence group goals and the freedom to contribute to them. With this process in operation, you can concentrate on solving the problems that interfere with goal attainment and building work-group identity.

Areas of Involvement

In the course of fulfilling your role of supervisor, four areas of involvement need your attention: providing support, promoting interaction, emphasizing goals, and facilitating task accomplishment.

157

Providing Support. This area of involvement includes the things you do to increase or maintain each group member's sense of personal worth and importance as a team member. Included in this area are such things as providing encouragement and recognition for good performance, speaking out on behalf of group members to higher management, and referring others directly to group members to answer questions or solve problems.

Promoting Interaction. This area of involvement includes the things you do to create or maintain a network of interpersonal relationships among group members. Included in this area are such things as sponsoring or encouraging group socials, holding work-group meetings, and arranging lunch breaks so group members can be together.

Emphasizing Goals. Work groups exist to deliver a product or service to their customers. This area of involvement includes the things you do to create a high level of awareness and commitment to that purpose, such as creating, changing, clarifying, and gaining acceptance of group goals. This typically is done best through the involvement and participation of group members.

Facilitating Task Accomplishment. This area of involvement includes the things you do to provide effective work methods, facilities, equipment, and schedules for accomplishing group goals. A large portion of this area is spent solving problems that your group experiences with other groups it interfaces with.

Sharing the Load

These four areas of involvement are essential for an effective team. However, all of the contribution to the group in these areas need not come solely from the supervisor. In fact, in highly effective groups the total amount of help provided each other by group members is at least as great as the amount provided by the supervisor. The supervisor's attitude and pattern of involvement tend to be mirrored in the behavior of group members. This usually results in a total contribution far in excess of what could be achieved by the supervisor alone.

Group-Centered Supervision

The social nature of work groups is often overlooked in the search for ways to increase group effectiveness. The approach to group-centered supervision presented here uses the group as a social system and utilizes its power to set and achieve high performance goals. In the process this approach also taps the talent of group members and frees them to contribute to group objectives.

This is not necessarily an easy job for supervisors. Working in a highly interactive mode is demanding and both emotionally and physically tiring. But the results make it worth the costs involved. Whether you are simply concerned about your own success, committed to organizational goals, fearful of losing your job, or simply enjoy the personal satisfaction of being a good supervisor, the best way to get what you want is to move to group-centered supervision.

The move to group-centered supervision is easier when you have confidence in your group's ability to get involved successfully. If you lack confidence at this point, begin by moving gradually toward more group involvement. As you experience success, your confidence will build and allow you to involve the group more.

As a result of your group-centered supervision, you can expect increased productivity, employee satisfaction, and acceptance of change. Byproducts of the process will be increased group cohesiveness, cooperation, morale, and responsibility toward the organization.

CONCLUSION

Being a member of a cohesive, productive team can be an exciting work experience. As supervisor, you set the stage for your group to develop into such a team.

Encourage team development by providing support, promoting interaction, emphasizing goals, and facilitating task accomplishment. Then, be willing to share goal setting, decision making, problem solving, and control with your group.

When you achieve an effective team everyone's job will be more enjoyable—including yours.

SUGGESTIONS
- Share with your group information on organizational plans and feedback on group performance.
- Involve the group, through staff meetings, in setting work group goals.
- Utilize small groups to solve problems and make recommendations for improved work group operations.

Appendix

Planning for Growth and Development

- Assessment and Development of Supervisory Skills
- Action Planning for Work Group Improvement
- Career Planning Guide

Planning for Growth and Development

Now that you have read this book, you probably have some ideas where you can improve your supervisory skills. Here are some ideas and tools to help your improvement effort.

As discussed in Chapter 8, planning is the key to accomplishing anything worthwhile. Your growth and development, as well as that of your work group, require careful planning in order to be completed successfully. This effort will provide those energizing and directive forces so essential to achievement. (You might find it helpful to read Chapter 8 again before moving into this activity.)

In planning your growth and development as a supervisor, keep in mind the following three principles:

Everyone's Development Is Self-Development. Your company naturally has an interest in your growth and development. It probably will help you, but it cannot develop you. The motivation, desire, effort, interest, and responsibility must come from you. Both the obligation and the responsibility for development rest with the individual.

Most Development Is the Result of Day-to-Day Work Experiences. Very little development of people in business and industry occurs in the classroom. Most occurs on the job. You learn by facing the problems of daily life with an inquiring attitude. As problems occur, seek answers on how to handle them. Do not hesitate to ask for help and then take action. No training or development program can remove all of the risk. At best, it will only point in a general direction.

Development Should Focus on a Current Assignment. Your goal should be to do your present job particularly well. Focus your development on what is required to accomplish that. After all, performance in your present assignment becomes the basis for recommendations for promotion. While focusing on your present assignment, however, do not entirely neglect the future. Have some idea of where you want to go and how to get there.

PLANNING AIDS

Three forms are provided for your use in planning your growth and development. Form I guides you through an assessment of your knowledge and skills as a supervisor. It then directs your attention to planning for improvement in the areas you think need it. Form II directs your attention to your work group—your role in the group, relationships within the group, overall effectiveness. After identifying problems that exist, change strategies are developed. Finally, Form III directs your attention to your future. Where do you want to go? How do you get there?

You should be involved in only one of these development areas at a time. When you are confident of your abilities as a supervisor, turn to work-group development. When you have both of these under control, look to the future.

Assessment and Development of Supervisory Skills

This planning form focuses your attention on the knowledge and skills required to be a successful supervisor. By completing it, you will identify areas where you need improvement and then will develop plans to attain the improvement needed. Please complete the steps in the order presented.

SECTION 1—TECHNICAL KNOWLEDGE

Step A. Evaluate your knowledge of the work performed by your group. Have you kept up-to-date?

LOW | **1** | **2** | **3** | **4** | **5** | **HIGH**

Step B. If you rated yourself less than 5, in what areas do you need to improve your knowledge? List these areas below:

1. _____
2. _____
3. _____
4. _____
5. _____

Step C. Now develop an action plan to get the knowledge you need. List below, in order of priority, the steps you plan to take. (For example, attend a training session, read material, talk with someone, etc.)

Action Step   **Target Date**

1. _____   _____

(Step C continued)

2. _____   _____

_____

3. _____   _____

_____

4. _____   _____

_____

5. _____   _____

_____

SECTION 2—ADMINISTRATIVE DUTIES

Step A. Evaluate your knowledge of your administrative duties. How well do you know the policies and procedures for handling the accounting, purchasing, and personnel responsibilities that are part of your job?

LOW | **1** | **2** | **3** | **4** | **5** | **HIGH**

Step B. If you rated yourself less than 5, in what areas do you need to improve your knowledge? List these areas below:

1. _____

2. _____

3. _____

4. _____

5. _____

Step C. Now develop a plan of action to get the knowledge you need. List below, in priority, the steps you plan to take.

Action Step   **Target Date**

1. _____   _____

_____

(Step C continued)

2. _____   _____

_____

3. _____   _____

_____

4. _____   _____

_____

5. _____   _____

_____

SECTION 3—SUPERVISORY RESPONSIBILITIES

Step A. Evaluate how well you handle each of the following duties.

DUTY	LOW 1	2	3	4	HIGH 5	DOES NOT APPLY
1. Monitoring and controlling group performance.						
2. Evaluating and reviewing performance.						
3. Providing feedback.						
4. Assigning and distributing work.						
5. Coordinating group operations.						
6. Providing technical assistance.						

	LOW			HIGH		
DUTY	1	2	3	4	5	DOES NOT APPLY
7. Training and developing work group members.						
8. Leading and motivating group members.						
9. Handling administrative duties.						
10. Maintaining group morale.						
11. Keeping your boss informed.						
12. Planning and setting priorities.						
13. Delegating.						
14. Handling discipline.						
15. Conducting meetings.						

Step B. List below, in priority order, those duties that you feel need developing. (The ones you rated 3 or less.)

1. _____

2. _____

3. _____

4. _____

5. _____

Step C. Now develop an action plan to develop your abilities listed in Step B.

Action Step	Target Date
1. _____	_____
_____	
2. _____	_____
_____	
3. _____	_____
_____	
4. _____	_____
_____	
5. _____	_____
_____	
6. _____	_____
_____	

SECTION 4—SUMMARY

Step A. If you have a training or personnel officer available, consider discussing your plans with that person in order to see that you have not overlooked something, such as company training programs or materials.

Scheduled date of discussion: _____

Step B. Now that you have completed this form, consider meeting with your boss and discussing it.

Scheduled date of discussion: _____

Step C. Do you need approval to spend money to accomplish any of these plans? If so, obtain it before starting your plan.

Date expense approval was obtained: _____

Action Planning for
Work Group Improvement

This form focuses on ways to improve the effectiveness of your work group. Take a few hours to examine your work group and develop a plan to improve its effectiveness. During this process concentrate on the ideas presented in this text.

This guide is divided into two parts: Problem Identification and Change Strategies. Please complete the steps in the sequence presented.

SECTION 1—PROBLEM IDENTIFICATION

Step A. Describe how you would like your work group to be; that is, how it would be in an ideal but attainable state. Consider your role in the group, relationships among group members, relationships with other groups, and the group's overall effectiveness or productivity.

_____

_____

_____

_____

_____

_____

Step B. Describe how your group is today in regard to the same issues you described in Step A.

_____

_____

_____

170

(Step B continued)

_____

_____

_____

_____

Step C. What changes are required to move your group from where it is today to where you would like it to be? (This represents the gap you must overcome.)

_____

_____

_____

_____

_____

_____

Step D. What road blocks must be overcome to accomplish the changes listed in Step C? (For example, acceptance and support by others, approval to make changes, or budgetary constraints.)

_____

_____

_____

_____

_____

_____

_____

_____

171

Step E. What will you gain if your change effort is successful?

_____

_____

_____

_____

_____

_____

SECTION 2—CHANGE STRATEGIES

Step A. Who needs to be involved with you, and to what extent, in completing this change program?

1. Superior: _____

_____

_____

_____

_____

2. Peers: _____

_____

_____

_____

_____

3. Subordinates: _____

_____

_____

_____

_____

Step B. What actual steps must be taken by whom and when to accomplish the desired change?

Action Steps	Responsible Party	Target Date
1. _____		
_____	_____	_____
2. _____		
_____	_____	_____
3. _____		
_____	_____	_____
4. _____		
_____	_____	_____
5. _____		
_____	_____	_____
6. _____		
_____	_____	_____
7. _____		
_____	_____	_____
8. _____		
_____	_____	_____
9. _____		
_____	_____	_____
10. _____		
_____	_____	_____

Career Planning Guide

How much influence should you have over your career? How much can you have? In today's world there are many more degrees of freedom than most people realize. Few, however, take advantage of this freedom. Many let their future be determined by happenstance rather than take an active role in shaping it in their own interest. Assuming you would like to have some say in the matter, this planning guide will help you look at what is important to you and how you can work toward an objective that will net you the most satisfaction from your career.

SECTION 1—CAREER OBJECTIVE IDENTIFICATION

Step A. Look back over your career and list three or four experiences that gave you the greatest satisfaction. Briefly describe why you felt good about each one.

1. _____

_____

2. _____

_____

3. _____

_____

4. _____

_____

Step B. Look back over your career and list three or four experiences that gave you the greatest dissatisfaction. Briefly describe why you felt bad about each one.

1. _____

174

(Step B continued)

2. _____

_____

3. _____

_____

4. _____

_____

Step C. Examine the data listed in Steps A and B and, supplementing them with other insight about yourself, list the conditions that must be satisfied for you to consider your career a success. (Examples: work location, type of work, extent of freedom, etc.)

_____   _____

_____   _____

_____   _____

Step D. Look into the future. What would you like to do with your career? What type of work would you like to be doing ten years from now?

_____

_____

_____

_____

Step E. Will achieving this objective satisfy the conditions identified in Step C? If not, what else needs to be considered, i.e., supplementing career with avocational interests or modifying your career objective?

_____

_____

_____

_____

175

SECTION 2—INVENTORY OF SKILLS

Step A. List those things you do well.

_____

_____

_____

_____

_____

_____

Step B. List those things you do poorly.

_____

_____

_____

_____

_____

_____

Step C. Consider your career objective identified in Section 1, Step D, and list those strengths that can be utilized in attaining that position.

_____

_____

_____

_____

_____

_____

Step D. Consider your career objective identified in Section 1, Step D, and list those things you do poorly that must be improved to attain that position.

_____

_____

_____

_____

_____

_____

_____

_____

_____

_____

SECTION 3—ACTION PLANNING

Good goals are SMART:

- Specific—A good goal says exactly what you want to accomplish.

- Measurable—Being specific helps make your goal measurable. You need something by which to gauge your progress and tell you when you have reached your goal.

- Action-oriented—When expressing your goals, use statements that have active-tense verbs and are complete sentences.

- Realistic—Good goals must be attainable yet should require you to do something that will let you grow and improve yourself.

- Time-limited—Do not direct your goal to some vague future time but select and set a reasonable time limit in which to accomplish it.

177

Step A. Identify two goals to work toward in developing strengths or overcoming weaknesses necessary to attaining your career objective.

1. _____

_____

2. _____

_____

Step B. Identify the people whose help you need in order to reach your career objective.

	Name	What You Need From Them
1.	_____	_____
2.	_____	_____
3.	_____	_____

Step C. Identify the action steps necessary to achieve your career objective—strengths to develop, weaknesses to overcome, relationships to promote. Consider the resources at your disposal and potential barriers you may encounter. Set a target date for completing each action step.

Action Step	Resources	Barriers	Target Date
1. _____	_____	_____	
_____	_____	_____	_____
2. _____	_____	_____	
_____	_____	_____	_____
3. _____	_____	_____	
_____	_____	_____	_____
4. _____	_____	_____	
_____	_____	_____	_____

If you have enjoyed this book, you will be pleased to know that we specialize in creative instructional books for both individual and professional growth.

Call or write for our free catalog.

CRISP LEARNING
1200 Hamilton Court
Menlo Park, CA 94025

TEL: 1-800-442-7477
FAX: 1-650-323-5800
Website: CrispLearning.com